CAMBRIDGE
Global English

Teacher's Resource

1

Annie Altamirano,
Caroline Linse and Elly Schottman

CAMBRIDGE
UNIVERSITY PRESS

CAMBRIDGE
UNIVERSITY PRESS

University Printing House, Cambridge CB2 8BS, United Kingdom

One Liberty Plaza, 20th Floor, New York, NY 10006, USA

477 Williamstown Road, Port Melbourne, VIC 3207, Australia

4843/24, 2nd Floor, Ansari Road, Daryaganj, Delhi – 110002, India

79 Anson Road, #06–04/06, Singapore 079906

Cambridge University Press is part of the University of Cambridge.

It furthers the University's mission by disseminating knowledge in the pursuit of education, learning and research at the highest international levels of excellence.

Information on this title: www.cambridge.org

First published 2014

20 19 18 17 16 15 14 13 12 11 10

Printed in Great Britain by CPI Group (UK) Ltd, Croydon CR0 4YY

A catalogue record for this publication is available from the British Library

ISBN 978-1-107-64226-3 Teacher's Resource

Additional resources for this publication at www.cambridge.org/

Cambridge University Press has no responsibility for the persistence or accuracy of URLs for external or third-party internet websites referred to in this publication, and does not guarantee that any content on such websites is, or will remain, accurate or appropriate. Information regarding prices, travel timetables, and other factual information given in this work is correct at the time of first printing but Cambridge University Press does not guarantee the accuracy of such information thereafter.

Contents

Map of the Learner's Book

Listening/Speaking	School subjects	Phonics / Word study	Critical thinking / Values
Listen to letters, numbers and colours	Maths: Number review	Alphabet review	

Listen for information
Listen to letters
Interviews
Discuss, act out poems and songs
	Geography	Letter names
		Spelling
		Capital letters
		Labels
			Understanding and conducting
			  interviews
			Organising and making charts
			Making friends, working, playing
			  and learning together

Listen for information
Ask and answer
Talk about families
Discuss, act out poems and songs
	Maths: 1–10, simple
	  problem solving
	Geography
	Social studies
		th
		Short a
		Rhyming words
			Families in different parts of the world
			Asking survey questions, creating and
			  discussing graphs
			Classification
			How families work and play together

Listen to / give instructions
Make a new song verse
Discuss and act out poems, songs,
  stories
	Physical education	Short u
		Rhyming words
		Question marks
		Read and act out
		  decodable story
			What games can we play?
			Creative problem solving
			Compare and contrast
			Taking turns, speaking politely,
			  being a good sport

Listen for information
Ask and talk about pictures
Discuss and act out poems, songs,
  stories
	Arts and crafts
	Shapes and colours
	Make puppets
		Short e
		I'm (contractions)
		Rhyming words
			What can we make with colours
			  and shapes?
			Recognising and reproducing
			  word patterns
			Planning and making a quilt
			Helping others
			Cleaning up after ourselves

Interviews
Guided speaking
Discuss and act out stories, poems,
  songs
Sing new verses
Ask and answer information questions
	Science: Life cycles
	Growing vegetables
		Short i, ch, sh
		Tongue twisters
		Identify rhyming words
		I'm/we're (contractions)
			What can you find on a farm?
			Document growth of seeds
			Interpreting diagrams
			Story maps
			Taking care of plants and animals
			  is important

Talk about ability Talk about senses Act out a story	Music Science: Senses Arts and crafts: Making instruments	Short o -er forms Compare minimal pairs Rhyming sounds	How do we use our five senses? Making lists Comparing things Understanding high and low sounds Inclusion/awareness of disability Respecting differences

Listen for information
Talk about transportation
  and movement
Listen to stories, poems
Song
	Arts and crafts: Making
	  a helicopter
	Science: Hands-on
	  exploration, shapes
		Long e sound
		Listen for sounds
			How do we travel around?
			Classifying and identifying difference
			  between vehicles and movement
			Keeping safe while using
			  transportation

Listening comprehension
Guided speaking
Dialogues
Emphatic expression
Discuss and act out stories, poems,
  songs
	Science and the
	  environment
	Weather patterns
	Experiment: Things that
	  float
		Long a spellings ai and ay
		Punctuation and capitals
			Why is water important?
			Providing examples to support ideas
			Predicting outcomes
			Understanding nature and survival
			Understanding the importance
			  of water

Listening comprehension: Routes
Talk about where you live
Act out conversation
Play games
Perform poems
Ask for and give things
	Social studies: Living in
	  cities
		-y endings
		Awareness of syllables
		Rhyming words
			What can you see, hear and do in
			  a city?
			Interpreting maps
			Interpreting poems
			We can appreciate where we live
			We can respect different opinions

Introduction

Welcome to *Cambridge Global English Stage 1*

Cambridge Global English is an eight-stage course for learners of English as a second language. The eight stages range from the beginning of primary to the penultimate year of junior secondary (roughly ages 6–13). The course has been designed to fulfil the requirements of the Cambridge English as a Second Language curriculum framework developed by Cambridge English Language Assessment. These internationally recognised standards provide a sequential framework for thorough coverage of basic English concepts and skills.

The materials reflect the following principles:

- *An international focus*. Specifically developed for young learners throughout the world, the themes, situations and literature covered by *Cambridge Global English* strive to reflect this diversity and help learners find out about each other's lives through the medium of English. This fosters respect and interest in other cultures and leads to awareness of global citizenship.
- *An enquiry-based, language-rich approach to learning*. *Cambridge Global English* engages children as active, creative learners. As learners participate in a wide variety of curriculum-based activities, they simultaneously acquire content knowledge, develop critical thinking skills and practise English language and literacy. The materials incorporate a 'learning to learn' approach, helping children acquire skills and strategies that will help them approach new learning situations with confidence.
- *English for educational success*. To meet the challenges of the future, children need to develop facility with both conversational and academic English. From the earliest level, *Cambridge Global English* addresses both these competencies. *Cambridge Global English* presents authentic listening and reading texts writing tasks and culminating unit projects similar to those learners might encounter in English-medium and international schools. Emphasis is placed on developing the listening, speaking, reading and writing skills learners will need to be successful in using authentic English-language classroom materials. At Stage 1, very basic learning strategies are introduced and practised. These lay the foundations for future language learning and development.
- *Rich vocabulary development*. Building a large and robust vocabulary is a cornerstone to success in both conversational and academic English. *Cambridge Global English* exposes learners to a wide range of vocabulary. Many opportunities for revising these words and using them in personalised, meaningful ways are woven into the activities and lesson plans.

- *Individualised learning*. We approach learning in an individual way by both acknowledging the individual nature of the knowledge and background of each child and encouraging their specific input. We also provide for differentiated learning in the classroom by offering a range of activities of varying difficulty and extra challenges. Unit by unit support for this is provided in the unit notes in this book.
- *Integrated assessment*. Throughout the course, teachers informally assess their learners' understanding of language and concepts. The Teacher's Resource provides suggestions for extending or re-teaching language skills based on learners' demonstrated proficiency. At the end of each unit, learners apply the skills and knowledge they have acquired as they work in groups to create and present a project of their choice. This provides teachers with an excellent performance assessment opportunity. An end-of-unit quiz in the Activity Book provides another evaluation measure: a quick progress check on learners' understanding of key ESL and early literacy skills.

Cambridge Global English can be used as a stand-alone ESL curriculum, or it can be used as part of an innovative suite of materials created by Cambridge University Press for young learners at international primary schools:

- *Cambridge Primary Science*
- *Cambridge Primary Mathematics*
- *Cambridge Primary English (L1)*
- *Cambridge Global English*.

We encourage you to learn more about these complementary courses through the Cambridge University Press website: education.cambridge.org

We hope that you and your learners will enjoy using these materials as much as we enjoyed developing them for you.

The *Cambridge Global English* team

A Components

Cambridge Global English offers the following components:

- The **Learner's Book** provides the core input of the course and consists of nine thematic units of study. Each unit contains six lessons developed around a unifying theme, and linked to a main question at the beginning of the unit. The materials cater for the needs of learners studying in a primary context: they feature skills-building tasks for listening, reading, writing and speaking, as well as language focuses. In addition, there is a strong vocabulary-building element to the course. Ways of introducing basic learning awareness skills are also explored through features such as:
  - Language tips
  - Words to remember
  - Language detective
  - Look what I can do!

  Materials are aimed at the learner with all the experiences that they bring to the classroom. Learners are encouraged to see the moral and social values that exist in many of the course texts, and find opportunities to reflect on these. We feel that the learner needs to be exposed to many different forms of text topics and styles in order to develop the skills of assessing, interpreting and responding appropriately to content. Therefore the course aims to provide a variety of factual and fictional texts, dialogues and poetry, on a range of different topics, at the appropriate level.
- The **Audio CDs** include all the listening material needed for the Learner's Book and Activity Book. The listening material supports the Learner's Book with listening, pronunciation and phonics activities, as well as songs and read-along stories. We recommend that learners also use the Audio CDs at home to practise the songs and stories, and to show their parents what they know.
- The **Activity Book** provides additional practice activities, deepening the understanding of language skills and content material introduced in the Learner's Book.
- The **Teacher's Resource** provides valuable guidance and support for using *Cambridge Global English* in your classroom. We understand that within each class there are learners of different abilities, particularly at Stage 1 when children come from different pre-primary backgrounds. It is very important to support differentiated work in the classroom and we do this through suggestions in the unit notes and additional differentiation 'challenge' activities in the Activity Book. The production skills required in the project work at the end of each unit can also be graded in terms of ability.

At the end of the Teacher's Resource, photocopiable activities, cross-referenced in the unit notes, are provided to give additional work for each lesson. A selection of lesson-by-lesson spelling words, which can be photocopied, cut out and given to the children to learn, are also included in the end section.

B Learner's Book structure

Cambridge Global English consists of nine thematic units of study, designed to cover approximately three units per term, in most educational systems. The Stage 1 Learner's Book is structured as follows:

- **Starter unit:** At the beginning of primary school, learners can come from a variety of backgrounds. Ideally most will have had some basic introduction to letters and numbers in English before they start this course, but a Starter unit is still included at the beginning of the Learner's Book to provide an opportunity to review these basic concepts. The Teacher's Resource offers a range of further activity suggestions for providing learners with additional support and basic language practice, so that they can all approach the Stage 1 Learner's Book with confidence.
- **Main units:** Nine thematic units provide a year's worth of curriculum lessons.
- **Picture dictionary:** At the end of the book there is a thematically arranged Picture dictionary. This dictionary can be used for a number of activities, such as reviewing material at the end of terms, but its main aim is to introduce the concept of using a dictionary in order to look up the meaning of words. This should be done on a fairly regular basis, so that the learners become accustomed to the idea.

C Unit structure

Each unit is divided up into six lessons. The length of lessons will vary from school to school, so a strict time limit for each lesson has not been prescribed. Lessons are structured as follows:

- **Lesson 1 Think about it:** Lesson 1 introduces the main topic, usually in the form of a question which should be a trigger for input from the learners in line with the enquiry-led approach of the course. A short poem and main picture lead into the topic of the unit, giving learners an opportunity to identify key vocabulary items. This leads to vocabulary practice tasks and culminates in a productive task.
- **Lesson 2 Find out more:** Lesson 2 is geared to deeper learning about a curriculum topic. It usually involves a short listening or reading passage followed by critical thinking skills and guided writing tasks.

- **Lesson 3 Letters and sounds:** Lesson 3 focuses on the mechanics of reading and pronunciation, including phonics, alphabet skills, reading, listening and writing skills. It usually contains a song or simple phonics story.
- **Lesson 4 Use of English:** Lesson 4 focuses on developing language skills through contextualised activities. It involves combinations of speaking, writing and reading activities.
- **Lesson 5 Read and respond:** Lesson 5 focuses on literacy and reading stories, poems and factual texts. It allows the learner to explore a variety of text types and develop comprehension and writing skills through related activities.
- **Lesson 6 Choose a project:** Lesson 6 is the consolidation and production section of the unit. Learners produce a project related to the unit content. Lesson 6 begins with a restatement of the initial unit question and leads to a review of what has been learned in the course of the unit. Learner independence is enhanced by allowing choice. Learners choose one of three projects to complete. At the end of the lesson they carry out a short activity (*Look what I can do!*) where learners can be encouraged to identify and demonstrate skills they have accumulated during the course of the unit.

D Activity Book

Each lesson in the Learner's Book is supported by two Activity Book pages that reinforce learning through activities, clearly framed within the 'I can' objectives of the course. The Activity Book provides basic practice and reinforcement of vocabulary, use of English, writing and concepts. It also provides opportunities for personalisation and creative work, as well as activities that can offer a higher level of challenge to support differentiated classroom situations. The last lesson of each unit in the Activity Book is devoted to an end-of-unit quiz, offering more in-depth assessment of what the learners have achieved.

E Customising your lessons

Support for planning each lesson and teaching objectives are provided in the main unit notes of this book. When planning, please also bear in mind the following:

- These are ideas and guidelines only; you should adapt them to your situation and the needs of your learners. Do not be afraid of changing things and bringing in to the classroom additional elements of your own.
- Monitor your learners. If they need additional support for some aspect of the book or particular skills work, tailor the material to their needs.

- Learners of this age group need repetition and revision. Do not be afraid of going over material several times. We would encourage you to continue singing songs, reading stories and playing games throughout the year. Create routines and chants that learners can join in with.
- Be creative in developing craft activities and role-plays. Some suggestions are given but there is much more that can be done. Try combining English with arts and crafts classes.
- Try to encourage learning/teaching/showing between classes of different age groups.
- Draw on parental support where possible. There are 'home–school link' suggestions in every unit.

When using the book, the following guidelines might also be useful:

Before using the Learner's Book
- Engage in warm-up activities (songs, total physical response (TPR), vocabulary games, alphabet chants, etc.).
- Pre-teach and practise key language learners will encounter in the Learner's Book and Audio CDs.

While using the Learner's Book
- Keep learners actively engaged.
- Use the artwork in Lesson 1 as a conversation starter: ask learners to name everything they see in the picture; play *I Spy,* etc.
- Vary the group dynamics in the lesson: move from whole group response to individual response to pairwork, etc.
- Provide opportunities for learners to ask questions as well as answer them.
- Encourage learners to act out the language in the lessons.
- Encourage learners to use language structures and vocabulary to talk about their own ideas, opinions and experiences.
- In class discussions, write the learners' ideas on class charts. You can refer back to these charts in later lessons.
- Adjust your reading and writing expectations and instructions to suit the literacy level of your learners.

Using the Activity Book and further suggestions
- Use the Activity Book pages related to the Learner's Book pages.
- Depending on the ability of the learners, use the 'Additional support and practice' activities and/or 'Extend and challenge' activities suggested in the Teacher's Resource at the end of every lesson.
- Do a wrap-up activity or game at the end of every lesson.

---

1 Welcome to school

Unit overview

In this unit learners will:

- Identify and describe objects in their classroom
- Greet each other and introduce themselves
- Talk about what they do at school
- Learn about ways children go to school
- Ask each other simple questions
- Introduce a new friend.

Learners will build communication and literacy skills as they go on a classroom treasure hunt, write their name, age and favourite colour, interview partners, create a class graph, and recite and act out an ABC chant, a spelling song and a story poem.

At the end of the unit, they will apply and personalise what they have learned by completing a project of their choice: making word cards for the **Word wall**, writing an original poem or creating a colour book.

Language focus

Singular and plural nouns: *chair, chairs*

Present simple: positive statements: *I go to school. We sing.*

Possessive adjectives: *my, his, her*

Adjective order: *a blue pencil*

Vocabulary topics: people, objects, colours, activities in school, greetings and introductions, numbers, letters of the alphabet

Critical thinking

- Analysing the characteristics of a poem versus a story
- Organising information into charts
- Comparing themselves to other children
- Assessing similarities and differences.

Self-assessment

- I can say the names of things in my classroom.
- I can say what I do at school.
- I can write my name.
- I can read and write the letters of the alphabet.
- I can introduce a friend.

Teaching tips

Study skill: using the book as a resource for learning.
Tell learners that if they have difficulty writing any new words, they can look for them in the Learner's Book and copy from there. Explain that their book is a resource for learning and they can use it for help in completing the exercises.

It is important to provide opportunities for peer correction and pair work. This interaction fosters cooperation and attention to detail.

Review the learners' work on the quiz, noting areas where they demonstrate strength and areas where they need additional instruction and practice. Use this information to customise your teaching as you continue to **Unit 2**.

If possible, leave the learner projects on display for a short while, then consider filing the projects, photos or scans of the work, in learners' portfolios. Write the date on the work.

Lesson 1: Think about it

What do we do at school?

Learner's Book pages: 10–11

Activity Book pages: 4–5

Lesson objectives

Listening: Listen to a poem and a conversation, follow directions, listen for information.

Speaking: Have a conversation with a friend, practise theme vocabulary.

Reading: Recite and read a poem, read classroom labels (theme vocabulary) and a treasure hunt list.

Writing: Write *yes* and *no,* write numbers, select and write words to complete an original poem.

Critical thinking: Analyse the differences between a poem versus a story, organise information into charts.

Language focus: Singular and plural nouns: *chair, chairs;* possessive adjectives: *my, your;* adjective order: *a blue pencil*

Vocabulary: *school, table, chairs, books, pencils, rulers, crayons, lunchbox, clock, door, whiteboard, alphabet chart, computers, friend* (colour, number, alphabet review)

Materials: Large sheets of paper and markers; classroom objects or pictures: book, pencil, ruler, lunchbox, crayon; a set of word labels for vocabulary items above; Classroom rules poster (use the illustration on Learner's Book page 10 or make a larger version).

Learner's Book

☞ Warm up

- Ask each learner: *What's your name?*
- Ask the class to clap and chant a variation on the Welcome chant (using learners' names), Teacher's Resource, page 19. At the end of each verse, learners wave and say: *Thank you!*
- Who are we? Talk about the different learners. Ask: *Are we all the same? How are we different?* Elicit answers from the class.

☞ Introduce vocabulary

- Use objects or pictures to introduce *book, pencil, ruler, lunchbox, crayon.*
- Say: *Look and listen.* Hold up each object, say the word. Learners repeat after you.
- Attach word labels to classroom items. Then point to the object and ask: *What's this?*
- Introduce a Classroom rules poster as *a list of rules* (See Learner's Book page 10 for poster reference). Learners repeat *Look and listen* as they point to their eyes and ears. Then they say and act out the rest of the poster.

1 Read and listen ③

- Open books at page 10. Learners point to and name objects they see in the picture. Write the objects they name on a chart on the board or a large piece of paper. Add a small sketch after each word. Together, read the chart.
- Point to the poem. Say: *Read and listen.*
- Play the audio a few times. Pause for learners to repeat each line and point to the objects in the picture.
- Practise reciting the poem together as you point to the objects in your classroom.
- **Critical thinking:** Ask learners to read the poem again and ask what makes a poem, e.g. rhyming words, text divided into lines. Ask them to find the two words that rhyme: *school* and *rules.*

Audioscript: Track 3

Speaker: *Hello, school!*

Tables and chairs

A list of rules

Books and crayons

Hello, school!

2 What's in the classroom?

- Point to the small pictures. Say: *Find a blue pencil.* Learners find a blue pencil in the big picture and repeat the words: *A blue pencil.* Repeat for *a green ruler* and *a red lunchbox.*
- Ask the learners to find additional objects: *a yellow pencil, a black crayon, a purple book, a yellow chair.*

3 🗨 Making friends ④

- Learners look at page 10. Introduce the two girls in the picture (Anna on the left, and Maria on the right).
- Say: *Listen. How old are the children?* Play the audio. Point to each girl as you listen to her lines.
- Hold up six fingers when Anna says, *I'm six.*
- Play the audio again. Pause and have learners repeat each line.
- Divide the class into two groups. Play the audio again. Group A repeats Anna's lines. Group B repeats Maria's lines. Switch roles and repeat.

Audioscript: Track 4

Anna: Hi. I'm Anna. What's your name?

Maria: My name is Maria. How old are you?

Anna: I'm six.

Maria: Me too!

Anna: I like your lunchbox.

Maria: Thank you!

Answers
Anna and Maria are six years old.

4 Topic vocabulary

- Focus on page 11. Direct learners' attention to the words. Play the audio and make the meanings clear.
- Write the words on the board. Read the words together. Draw attention to the plural ending -s.
- Learners look at the picture. Ask: *How many chairs? Let's count. One, two. How many computers?*
- Place word labels by classroom objects. Say the words together as a class.

Audioscript: Track 5
Speaker: a table

a clock

a whiteboard

an ABC chart

chairs

computers

5 Classroom treasure hunt 6

- Point to the boy in the picture. Say: *This is Matteo. He is doing a classroom treasure hunt. Look at the picture. Which thing does he forget to say?*
- Play the audio several times to help learners discover the answer.
- **Critical thinking:** Explain that you use a table or a chart to organise information. Ask: *How many columns and rows are there in this chart?* What other types of information can learners organise in this way?

Audioscript: Track 6
Matteo: In my classroom, there are tables and chairs. There are lots of books, and two computers. There's also a whiteboard. What do you have in your class?

Answer
a clock

[AB] For further practice, see Activities 1 and 2 in the Activity Book.

6 School poem

- Recite the *Hello, school!* poem together again. Tell learners that they will now write their own school poem as a class.
- Copy the poem skeleton from Activity Book page 5 onto a large sheet of paper or the board:
Hello, school!
_____ *and* _____
A list of rules
_____ *and* _____
Hello, school!
- Learners choose a school object to write on each line. Read the poem together.

[AB] For further practice, see Activity 3 in the Activity Book.

Wrap up

- Write *Things in our classroom* on a large piece of paper or the board. Ask: *What's in our classroom?* Write words the learners say on the chart.

Activity Book

1 Classroom treasure hunt

- Preview the treasure hunt list. Learners colour in the first three items (chair, pencil and book).
- Answer the first item as a class. Learners then work in pairs to complete the list.

Answers
Learners' own answers.

2 Count and write

- Direct learners' attention to **Activity 2**. Explain the activity. Check answers as a class.

Answers
1 2 rulers **2** 4 pencils **3** 3 books **4** 2 boys **5** 4 girls

3 Write your own *Hello, school!* poem

- Learners now write and illustrate a poem of their own. Invite learners to read their poems aloud.
- **Critical thinking:** Direct learners' attention to the completed poem on page 10 of the Learner's Book. Ask learners about the differences between poems and stories. Show them a story and a poem to compare the structures. They compare them and find the differences, e.g. poems are written in verses that may rhyme or not, and each verse goes on a different line. A story is written as continuous text and does not rhyme. Ask them if they know the names of any poems or stories in their own language.

Answers
Learners' own answers.

I can say the name of things in my classroom.

Direct learners' attention to the self-evaluation question at the top of page 4. Ask them to think and answer. Emphasise the importance of giving an honest answer.

Answers
Learners' own answers.

Differentiated instruction

Additional support and practice

- 'Getting to know you' conversations
- Lead a chain conversation. Learner A: *What's your name?* Learner B: *My name is (Paula).* Learner A: *How old are you?* Learner B: *I am (six).* Class: *Hello, (Paula)!* Learner B: *Hello!*
- Learners stand at the front of the room. Give each an object. They say: *(Irena), I like your (lunchbox).* Cue the learner to respond: *Thank you!*

Extend and challenge

- 🗣 **Vocabulary concentration:** Give each learner eight index cards. They write and illustrate eight vocabulary words. In pairs, lay cards face down; four rows of four cards. They take turns turning over two cards, one at a time, saying the words aloud. If two matching cards are turned over, the player keeps the pair of cards. If the cards do not match, the player turns them face down again and it is the next player's turn.

Lesson 2: Find out more

Children around the world

Learner's Book pages: 12–13

Activity Book pages: 6–7

Lesson objectives

Listening: Listen and respond to informational text.

Speaking: Have a conversation with a friend, practise theme vocabulary.

Reading: Read informational text, read and discuss a chart.

Writing: Complete sentences to give information about yourself: name, age, favourite activity. Use capital letters to write names.

Critical thinking: Learners compare themselves to other children, assessing similarities and differences.

Language focus: Positive statements: *I go to school. We sing.* Information questions: *What do you do at school? How do you go to school?* Present simple tense; *I, we, you.*

Vocabulary: *read, do Maths, write, use computers, draw, sing, walk, bus, car, bicycle, boat*

Materials: One copy of **Photocopiable activity 2** for each learner, large sheets of paper and markers; six word cards with small pictures for the verbs given on page 12 of the Learner's Book; *Hello, school!* class poem from Lesson 1; blank reproduction of chart from Learner's Book page 13; learners' names written on strips of paper.

Learner's Book

🖙 Warm up

- Clap your hands to the beat as you say and act out the Welcome chant, version 1 (Teacher's Resource page 19).
- Review the names of classroom objects. Point to different objects and say: *What's this?*

🖙 🔢 Let's do Maths!

- Write on the board: *1 + 1 =.* Say: *Let's do Maths. One and one is …* Learners raise hands to answer.

- A volunteer writes the answer on the board. The class repeat: *One and one is two.*
- Draw groups of objects, e.g. five pencils and eight chairs. Ask learners to decide in which group there are more objects.
- Do more sums to practise numbers one to ten.

🖙 TPR: Introduce vocabulary

- Introduce the verbs using the word cards. Say the word and mime the action. Learners repeat.
- Point to yourself and say: *I.* Then say: *I (read) at school.* Learners repeat.
- Gesture to include the whole class as you say: *We.* Then say: *We (read) at school.* Learners repeat.
- **Mime game:** Say: *Guess the word.* Ask a volunteer to select one card to act out. The class guess the word, then act it out. Ask: *What do you do at school?* Class answer: *We (sing) at school.* Learners then act *We sing at school.*

1 Before you read 🔢

- Open books at page 12. Point to each photo. Say: *This* (girl's / boy's) *name is* (learner's name). *What does* (learner's name) *do at school?* Learners answer with a verb or verb phrase: *use computers, read, do Maths.*
- Play the audio. Point to the pictures in turn. Play the audio again, pausing to allow learners to repeat each line. Learners follow the words in their book.
- Ask learners to read the lines individually or in pairs.

Audioscript: Track 7

Amira: My name is Amira.
I am six.
I use computers at school.

Marat: My name is Marat.
I am seven.
I read at school.

Zak: My name is Zak.
I am six.
I do Maths at school.

Answers
1 Amira uses computers at school.
2 Marat reads at school.
3 Zak does Maths at school.

Writing tip

- Ask learners to look at the words in the sentences under each picture and ask why they think some words are written in a different way, e.g. Amira, Zak, Marat.
- Read the **Writing tip** aloud. Explain *capital letter.* Hand each learner a strip of paper with their name on it. Ask: *What capital letter does your name begin with?*

2 What do you do at school?

- Point to each of the six vocabulary pictures. Ask: *What do you do at school?* Learners respond.
- Direct their attention to the writing activity. Model the answer with one of the learners.
- Ask individual learners to say the complete sentences to the class.

> **Answers**
> Learners' own answers.

 For further practice, see Activity 1 in the Activity Book.

3 How do children go to school? 8

- Use the photos to introduce the new vocabulary. Point to each photo, say the word and mime. Learners repeat the word and action.
- Ask: *How do children go to school?* Point to yourself and say: *I go by bicycle.* Pretend to ride a bicycle. Learners repeat and mime.
- Invite several learners to join you and pretend to ride a bicycle. Gesture to the group and say: *We go by bicycle.*
- Have the class repeat and mime. Repeat with the other four photos.
- Play the audio. Point to the picture that goes with the words. Play the audio again, pausing to allow learners to repeat each line.
- Read the sentences out at random. Learners point to the matching picture and repeat the sentence.
- **Critical thinking:** Ask learners to look at the pictures and compare what children do in other countries with what they do themselves. How similar or different are they?

> **Audioscript:** Track 8
> **Boy:** I go by bicycle.
> **Children:** We go by bus.
> **Girl:** I go by car.
> **Children:** We go by boat.
> **Boys:** We walk.

> **Answers**
> By bicycle, bus, car, boat and walking

4   A class chart

- Draw attention to the chart in the Learner's Book, page 13. Read the chart title and the words in the first row. Ask: *How many children go to school by bus? Let's count.*
- Repeat these steps with the next three rows. Introduce the chart and name strips, and tell learners they are going complete their own class chart.

> **Answers**
> Learners' own answers.

 For further practice, see Activity 2 in the Activity Book.

Wrap up

- Write the title *What do we do in school?* on a large piece of paper and ask children the question. Write the words the children say on the chart.
- **Home–school link:** Learners show page 7 of their Activity Books to parents and explain what they did in class. They can also ask parents how they went to school when they were children and report back to the class the following day.

Activity Book

1 Write and draw

- Ask learners to complete the sentences about themselves and draw a picture.
- Hand name strips to children who need help in writing their names.

> **Answers**
> Learners' own answers.

2 A class chart

- Ask the learners questions about the chart on page 7. Read the first question in the Activity Book: *How many children go by bus?* Explain the example answer: *5.* Read the other questions with the learners. They write the answers. Provide help as needed.
- **Critical thinking:** Draw learners' attention to how the chart is organised and how to work with it.

> **Answers**
> 1 5
> 2 3
> 3 1
> 4 2

Challenge

- Focus on the questions. Elicit some answers from the class. Learners then write their answers. Circulate to help with spelling if necessary.

> **Answers**
> Learners' own answers.

I can say what I do in school. I can write my name.

- Direct learners' attention to the self-evaluation question at the top of page 6. Ask them to think and answer. Emphasise the importance of giving an honest answer.

> **Answers**
> Learners' own answers.

Differentiated instruction

Additional support and practice

- Give each learner a copy of **Photocopiable activity 2**. Do the counting activity as a class. Then learners trace the numbers. Focus on the pictures and ask learners to count how many of each object there are. They write their answers. Then ask them to compare if there are more children or more books.

Extend and challenge

- Read the captions under the photos on page 12. Ask: *Are any of the children from the country you are in? Are any from a nearby country? What is the name of your country in English?* Help learners locate the three countries on a map or globe. Trace the route from their country to each of these other countries.

Lesson 3: Letters and sounds

The alphabet

Learner's Book pages: 14–15
Activity Book pages: 8–9

Lesson objectives

Listening: Listen to a song and identify the letters of the alphabet.

Speaking: Recite an alphabet poem, sing a spelling song, make a new song.

Reading: Recognise letters of the alphabet, recognise the first letter of a word and its sound.

Writing: Write your name, write letters of the alphabet, spelling dictation.

Critical thinking: Classify words according to the initial letter, memorise a poem.

Language focus: Spelling names and words, information questions: *What do you see?* Present simple tense: *I see, we read …*

Vocabulary: Letters of the alphabet, *pen, hands, head, dog*

Materials: Chart with learners' names written on strips of paper (from **Lesson 2**); **Lesson 1** classroom labels: *books, table, computer, pencils, rulers, lunchbox, door, whiteboard*; a blank paper strip for each child; large capital letter cards *A–Z* (from Starter unit); ten blank cards for each child.

Learner's Book

Warm up

- Learners open their books at *The alphabet* on pages 6 and 7, and point to the letters as they join in the Alphabet song and the Alphabet chant they learnt in the **Starter unit**.
- Hold up a learner's name card. Ask: *Whose name is this? What's the first letter of* (learner's) *name?* Chant the first verse of the Welcome chant (see page 19),

swapping in the learner's name for 'children'. Repeat with several other names.

TPR: Put your hands on your head

- Introduce the words *hands* and *head* by holding up your hands and pointing to your head. Give TPR commands: *Put your hands on your head. Put your hands on (your chair / the table / your book / your pencil / your friend).*

1 Alphabet poem 9

- Learners turn to page 14. Point to the first row of alphabet letters in the alphabet poem. Say: *Let's read!* Chant the letters A to G together. Continue with the other rows of letters.
- Play the audio. Learners point to the letters as they listen and chant along.
- Play the audio again. Chant the words and mime. Pause after each line for learners to repeat the letters, words and gestures.
- Hand the letter cards A to G to seven learners. They arrange themselves in alphabetical order. Let the class chant the letters. Repeat with letters H to N, O to T and U to Z.
- Place all the letters in order in a row, and then remove several letters. Learners chant the alphabet. When they come to a gap, they choose the right letter to place in the gap.
- **Critical thinking:** Practise the poem until learners can memorise it. Then ask pairs or groups to recite it.

> **Audioscript:** Track 9
>
> **Boy:** A B C D E F G
>
> **Children:** We're in school, you and me.
>
> **Boy:** H I J K L M N
>
> **Children:** I have a pencil. You have a pen.
>
> **Boy:** O P Q, R S T
>
> **Children:** Look around. What do you see?
>
> **Boy:** U V W, X Y Z
>
> **Children:** Put your hands on your head!

AB For further practice, see Activity 1 in the Activity Book.

2 Word wall

- Point out the phrase *word wall* in the book. Ask: *How many names do you see under **Aa**? How many under **Bb**?*
- Learners make their own name cards. Circulate blank cards and ask: *What's the first letter in your name?* When name cards are completed, say: *Look at the first letter in your name. Is it A? Let's put names that begin with A on the word wall.* Continue through the alphabet.

> **Answers**
> Learners' own answers.

AB For further practice, see Activities 2 and 3 in the Activity Book.

3 📝 🎵 A spelling song 🔟

- Draw attention to the lettered juggling balls at the top of page 15. Point to the first ball. Ask: *What's this letter?* (B). Say: *Let's write the letter B in the air.*
- Learners copy your actions. Repeat with the remaining four balls.
- Give each learner five blank cards. Give directions as you model writing each letter on your own set of cards: *Write the letter (B).*
- Point out the *farmer* and the *dog* in the picture. Teach the words. Explain that the letters B-I-N-G-O spell *Bingo*, the name of the dog.
- Learners arrange their letter cards to spell BINGO. Practise saying and spelling the name aloud.
- Practise chanting the first verse of the song, line by line.
- Play the song and sing along, pointing to the letter cards. Stop the CD, explain that learners are to sing the song but clap once instead of saying *B*.
- Explain that in the next verse you will clap for the first two letters, in the following verse you will clap for three letters, then four letters; then finally all five letters. Practise doing this.
- Sing the song from the beginning. Sing and clap along.

> **Audioscript:** Track 10
> **Children:** There was a farmer had a dog
> And Bingo was its name-o.
> B-I-N-G-O! B-I-N-G-O! B-I-N-G-O!
> And Bingo was its name-o!
>
> There was a farmer had a dog
> And Bingo was its name-o.
> (*clap*)-I-N-G-O! (*clap*)-I-N-G-O! (*clap*)-I-N-G-O!
> And Bingo was its name-o!
>
> There was a farmer had a dog
> And Bingo was its name-o.
> (*clap, clap*)-N-G-O! ...
> And Bingo was its name-o!
>
> There was a farmer had a dog
> And Bingo was its name-o.
> (*clap, clap, clap*)-G-O! ...
> And Bingo was its name-o!
>
> There was a farmer had a dog
> And Bingo was its name-o.
> (*clap, clap, clap, clap*)-O! ...
> And Bingo was its name-o!
>
> There was a farmer had a dog
> And Bingo was its name-o.
> (*clap, clap, clap, clap, clap*) ...
> And Bingo was its name-o!

4 📝 🎵 Make a new song

- Point to the picture of children reading. Ask: *What do these children do in school?*
- Point to the letters. Say: *Yes, R-E-A-D spells read.* Learners spell the word. Repeat with the next picture.
- Sing the words of the READ verse to the tune of *Bingo*. Sing again, pausing for children to repeat.
- Show letter cards: *R, E A* and *D*. Point at each letter as you spell.

- Learners mix up the four letter cards and try to put the letters in the right order again to spell *READ*.
- Follow the same steps with the SING verse. Using the letter cards for BINGO and READ, ask what other letter learners need to make the word *SING*, and then show the letter card for *S*.

📖 For further practice, see Activity 4 in the Activity Book.

📤 Wrap up

- Pass out paper and pencils, markers or crayons. Learners write their name at the top of the paper, then write the alphabet using capital letters. Adjust this task to the skill level of the class. They can write just the first few letters or the whole alphabet. Collect, write the date on the back, and save in the learners' portfolio.

Activity Book

1 Capital letters

- After learners have practised the rhyme a few times focus on the activity and ask them to write the missing letters.
- When they have finished, check as a class.

> **Answers**
> C, F, I, K, M, P, S, W, Z

2 Trace and match

- Focus on the pictures and elicit the words from the class.
- Learners do the matching exercise independently. Check answers as a class.

> **Answers**
> | | | | |
> |---|---|---|---|
> | 1 | b | 5 | e |
> | 2 | a | 6 | h |
> | 3 | d | 7 | f |
> | 4 | c | 8 | g |

3 Word wall

- Focus on the words in the **Word box**. Explain the activity to the learners.
- Ask learners to work in pairs and classify the words into the correct category. Check answers as a class.
- **Critical thinking:** Classifying requires learners to identify and sort out according to a rule that they have to discover and apply. Ask learners to explain why they have classified the words in a certain way, e.g. *boy begins with B.*

> **Answers**
> Bb: *boy*   bus   book
> Cc: *computer*   clock   car

Challenge:

- Ask learners to add one more word to each category.

4 Mystery words

> **Answers**
> 1 table
> 2 pen
> 3 car

I can read and write the letters of the alphabet.

- Direct learners' attention to the self-evaluation question at the top of page 8. Ask them to think and answer. Emphasise the importance of giving an honest answer.

Differentiated instruction

Additional support and practice

- See letter and sound activities suggested in the Starter unit (Teacher's Resource page 19).

Extend and challenge

- Display the word cards from **Lesson 2**: *draw, read, write, sing*. Give learners spelling dictation, for example: D-R-A-W. Can they identify the word they have written?
- Add more letters to the word wall and ask learners to look in **Lessons 1–3** for words to include.

Lesson 4: Use of English

Favourite colours

Learner's Book pages: 16–17
Activity Book pages: 10–11

> ### Lesson objectives
> **Listening:** Listen to and follow directions, listen for specific information.
> **Speaking:** Interview a friend, introduce your friend (use the word *his* or *her*), spell your name aloud.
> **Reading:** Begin to read colour names.
> **Writing:** Write your name, your partner's name, and your favourite colours.
>
> **Language focus:** Possessive adjectives: *my, your, his, her*; *This is my friend. His/Her name is …; Can you spell your name, please?* Information questions: *What's your favourite colour?*
> **Vocabulary:** Colours *(review)*
>
> **Materials:** Crayons or markers in ten colours: red, yellow, blue, green, purple, orange, black, white, brown, pink; a collection of books, pens, pencils, toy cars, toy dogs and cats, lunchboxes, etc. of different colours; letter and word cards: *B, I, N, G, O, His* and *Her*; A4 sheets of paper.

Learner's Book

📖 Warm up

- Sit in a circle. Display the BINGO letter cards. Play the song. Sing and clap along. Ask several learners: *Can you spell the name Bingo, please?*
- Ask a learner: *Can you spell your name, please?* Write the letters on a piece of paper as the child spells. Ask the class: *Can you spell (Ahmed's) name?* Point to the letters as the class spells. Repeat with another name.

1 Colours 11

- Place a collection of coloured objects in the middle of the circle. Say: *Put your hand on something (red). Put your hand on something (brown).* Learners put their hands on the object.
- Open books at page 16. Play Track 11. Learners listen and point to the colours.
- Point to the words in the speech bubbles and pictures and read aloud. Learners repeat after you. Say: *Name something that is (blue).* Write learners' ideas on the board. Continue with all the colours.

> **Answers**
> *red, blue, green, yellow, brown, orange, black, purple, pink, white*

> **Audioscript:** Track 11
> **Speaker:** red
> blue
> green
> yellow
> brown
> orange
> black
> purple
> pink
> white

2 An interview 12

- Point to the picture of the girl with the clipboard interviewing the boy. Say: *This is Fatima. She is interviewing Ben. Fatima asks Ben three questions. Listen to Fatima. What questions does she ask?*
- Play the first interview several times. Write the questions on the board. Practise saying the questions.
- Say: *Ben spells his name. Listen and write Ben's name.* Play the interview again. Learners write Ben's name on a piece of paper.
- Ask: *What is Ben's favourite colour?* Point to Ben's name card. Read the information with learners: *Name: Ben. Favourite colour: black.*
- Point to the second name card with a picture of a girl (Lena). Say: *Fatima interviews another friend. Listen. What is her name? What is her favourite colour?*
- Play the audio several times. Learners listen and write the answers on a piece of paper. Discuss the answers together.

Answers
Fatima asks:
What's your name?
Can you spell your name, please?
What's your favourite colour?
Fatima's friend's name is *Lena* and her favourite colour is *pink*.

3 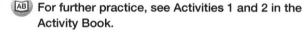 Make a name card

- Learners complete a name card by writing their name and favourite colour and drawing a picture of themselves (see Activity Book, page 10).
- **Home–school link:** Learners show the family the name cards they have made. They ask the same questions to parents and siblings and make similar cards for them.

4 Interview a friend

- Read the three questions with the class. Have learners choose two friends. They ask them the questions and write their answers.
- Partners stand up and introduce each other to the class, using the words they have written.
- Draw attention to the **Language detective** question: they will use the word *his* if their friend is a boy. If their friend is a girl, they will use the word *her*.

Answers
Learners' own answers.

For further practice, see Activities 1 and 2 in the Activity Book.

5 Mystery child

- Read the name and favourite colour on each name card with the learners. Say: *This is a girl. Her name begins with R. Her favourite colour is red. Can you find her?* Let children point to the matching name card. Invite a learner to describe another name card. Prompt as needed.
- Learners continue to play this game with a partner.

Answers
Learners' own answers.

For further practice, see Activity 3 in the Activity Book.

Wrap up

- **This is my friend:** Learners stand in a circle. Learner A joins hands with Learner B and they raise their hands in the air. Learner A introduces Learner B, beginning: *This is my friend … .* Then they drop their hands and Learner B repeats with the next learner in the circle. Continue until everyone has been introduced.

Activity Book

1 Name cards

- Explain the activity. Learners write the information on their name card and draw a picture. Then they do the same for their partner.

Answers
Learners' own answers.

2 Write about your friend

- Learners write the three sentences about their friend. Circulate, providing assistance with spelling if necessary.

Answers
Learners' own answers.

3 *His* and *her*

- Explain the activity. Read the sentences about Amy. Ask some comprehension questions: *What colour is her book? Is the chair green or yellow?* Learners then colour the picture. Repeat with the sentences for Tom.

I can introduce a friend.

- Direct learners' attention to the self-evaluation question at the top of page 10. Ask them to think and answer. Emphasise the importance of giving an honest answer.

Answers
Learners' own answers.

Differentiated instruction

Additional support and practice

- Learners choose a favourite fictional character and write a similar name card for them.

Extend and challenge

- Learners choose a friend, a family member or a fictional character and make a mini poster with a description following the model of **Activity 3** in the Activity Book.

Lesson 5: Read and respond

Learner's Book pages: 18–21
Activity Book pages: 12–13

Lesson objectives

Listening: Listen to and follow directions, listen to a story.
Speaking: Talk about the story, talk about what you see
Reading: Read along as you listen to the story, recognise the sight word *I*.
Writing: Write words in speech bubbles to complete a conversation.
Critical thinking: Predicting what happens in the poem by looking at pictures.

Language focus: *Hop like a rabbit. Swim like a duck. Climb like a squirrel;* present simple: affirmative sentences: *It swims. It hops;* information questions: *What do you see…? What do animals do?*
Vocabulary: *rabbit, duck, squirrel, hop, swim, climb*

Materials: Illustrated word cards: *rabbit, duck, squirrel;* a toy car, a toy dog, a lunchbox; a puppet (optional); pens, pencils, sheets of A4 paper.

Learner's Book

Warm up

- Use a puppet or toy animal to revise questions: *Hello! What's your name? How old are you? What's your favourite colour?*
- Play a few rounds of *Mystery child* from **Lesson 4**.

Introduce vocabulary

- Use word cards to introduce the *rabbit, duck* and *squirrel.* Ask: *What is the first letter in (rabbit)?*
- Learners mime animal movements. Say: *A rabbit hops. A duck swims. A squirrel climbs.* Write the verbs on the board.
- **Simon says:** Give the class instructions using simple actions for the verbs on the board. Learners should only do the action if the instruction is preceded by *Simon says,* e.g. *Simon says hop* (learners hop), *swim* (learners stay still).

1 Before you read 13

- **Critical thinking:** Read the title of the story. Learners look at the pictures to predict what the story will be about.
- Point to the pictures on pages 18, 19 and 20. Ask: *What does the girl see? What colour is the (rabbit, duck, squirrel)?*
- Point to picture 8 on page 20. Say: *The girl is at school. Is she neat and clean?* Mime to clarify words. *(No). Is she happy?* Grin to show the meaning of *happy.* *(Yes)*
- Play the audio. Point to the pictures in turn.
- Play the audio again, pausing to allow learners to repeat each line. Mime *little* with your hands.
- **Choral reading:** Learners follow the words in their book and read the sentence below each picture. Then invite individuals or pairs of learners to read the words aloud.

Audioscript: Track 13
See Learner's Book pages: 18–20.

Words to remember

- Write the word *I* on the board. Point to yourself as you say, *I.* Point out that the word *I* is always spelled with the capital letter I.
- Learners look for the sight word *I* in the story. How many times do they see the word? Have them count on their fingers. (seven)

2 Yes or no

- Ask: *What does the girl see on her way to school?* Point to each picture as you ask: *A duck? A bus? A rabbit? A squirrel?*
- Ask learners to look back at the story, then they answer *yes* or *no.* Ask them to show where these items appear in the story.

> **Answers**
> The girl sees a duck, a rabbit and a squirrel.

3 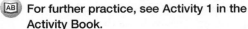 Over to you

- Point to the pictures. Ask: *What are these?* Review the vocabulary. Listen for pronunciation of the final /s/ sound in the plurals ending in –**s**.
- Ask: *What do <u>you</u> see on your way to school?* Help learners answer in a full sentence: *I see …*
- Learners tell their partners what they see on the way to school.

> **Answers**
> Learners' own answers.

[AB] **For further practice, see Activity 1 in the Activity Book.**

4 What do the animals do?

- Ask: *What do the animals do?* Point to the picture of the squirrel. Ask: *What's this? What does a squirrel do?* Trace a matching line with your finger from *A squirrel* to *climbs.*
- Say the start of the sentence and pause for learners to finish the sentence.
- Learners say the sentence as they mime. Repeat with the rabbit and the duck.

> **Answers**
> **1** A squirrel climbs. **2** A rabbit hops. **3** A duck swims.

[AB] **For further practice, see Activities 2 and 3 in the Activity Book.**

Wrap up

I can say a story poem

- Divide one class into four groups and ask each group to say two verses of the story poem. Then ask the class to name as many things they can see on their way to school as possible. Help with vocabulary as necessary.

Activity Book

1 Can you see it in the classroom or outside?

- Ask learners to look at the picture and decide which things they see inside and which outside. They draw lines to match the objects to the correct place.
- Ask them to then compare the picture with what they really see inside and outside their class.

> **Answers**
> clock – inside; table – inside; duck – outside;
> rabbit – outside; squirrel – outside

2 Word snake

- Focus on the word snakes. Explain how to find the words in them.
- Point at the pictures and the words and ask the class to say them aloud.
- Learners work independently to look for the words. They then check their answers with a partner.
- Check answers as a class.

> **Answers**
> **girl**mxkdurfu**pen**kyzqa**books**ventf
> mxrfuly**friends**bpwkrz**boy**qarti

3 What are the children saying?

- Focus on the pictures and ask learners to predict what the dialogue might be.
- Draw learners' attention to the **Word box** and ask them to complete the speech bubbles.
- They can then act out the dialogue in pairs.

> **Answers**
> What's your name? **My name is Paco**.
> How old are you? **I am 6**.
> I like your car. **Thank you!**

I can say the names of things in my classroom.

- Direct learners' attention to the self-evaluation question at the top of page 12. Ask them to think and answer. Emphasise the importance of giving an honest answer.

Differentiated instruction

Additional support and practice

- Bring in toy animals or pictures of animals (ducks, rabbits and dogs, for example) of different colours. Give TPR instructions: *Point to the (green duck)*. Learners sort the animals by colour. Ask: *How many yellow animals?* Learners identify each yellow animal: *a yellow duck, a yellow dog*, etc.
- Use a puppet to engage learners in conversation: *Hello! What's your name? How old are you? What's your favourite colour? I like your (duck)*. Learners use the puppet and ask each other the questions.

Extend and challenge

- 💬 Pairs of learners open their books to the School section of the **Picture dictionary** (page 137). They point to and say the words they know.
- **Early literacy: Silent TPR.** Write the words *hop, swim, climb,* and *walk* on four word cards.

  Point to the first letter and say, *What is the first letter of this word? What sound does (**h**) make? Let's say the word (hop). Do you hear the /h/ sound at the beginning of hop? Let's hop as we say the word hop.*

  Hold up the word cards in scrambled order. Have learners silently follow the commands.

Lesson 6: Choose a project

What do we do at school?

Learner's Book pages: 22–23
Activity Book pages 14–15

Lesson objectives

Listening: Listen to and follow directions, listen to comprehension items in the Activity Book quiz.

Speaking: Present your project to the class.

Reading: Read word cards, a poem, colour books, recognise letters in quiz.

Writing: Write word cards, a poem, or colour book captions, write name and letters in the Activity Book quiz.

Language focus: Unit 1 Review

Materials:

A Make word cards: Two to four blank word cards for each child; writing/drawing supplies; word cards from Lesson 5: *rabbit, duck, squirrel*.

B Write a poem: Template of poem with write-on line for verbs; word cards from **Lesson 2**: *read, do Maths, write, use computers, draw, sing*; writing/drawing supplies.

C Make a colour book: Writing/drawing supplies; word cards from Lesson 5: *rabbit, duck, squirrel*; camera (optional), printer (optional).

Learner's Book

☞ Warm up

- Play a game of *Simon says* to review action words: *Stand up. Raise your hand. Hop like a rabbit. Climb like a squirrel. Swim like a duck. Put your hands on your head. Put your hands on your chair. Sit down. Point to the (clock)*.

Choose a project

- Learners will choose an end-of-unit project to work on. Look at the learner-made samples and help them choose. Move the children into groups depending on their choices. Provide materials.

- **Informal assessment opportunity:** Circulate as learners work. Informally assess their receptive and productive language skills. Ask questions. You may want to take notes on their responses.

A Make word cards
- Read the directions in the Learner's Book. Each learner will make two to four word cards.
- Point to the word labels around room. Display the word cards from **Lesson 5**. Review the vocabulary pictures in **Lesson 1**, **Lesson 2**, and the School section in the **Picture dictionary** (page 137).

B Write a poem
- Read the directions. Read and practise the poem together.
- Display the word cards from **Lesson 2**. Show the template of the poem. Ask: *What do we do in school? Where can we find words?* (the word cards). Learners will also draw a picture to go with their poem.

C Make a colour book
- Read the directions. Ask: *What colours can you choose? What things can you draw?* Draw attention to the word labels around the room and the word cards from **Lesson 5**.

Look what I can do!
- Review the *I can …* statements. Learners demonstrate what they can do.

Activity Book

Unit 1 Quiz: Look what I can do!

Listen 91 [CD2 Track 38]
- For items 1–6, learners listen and tick the correct picture. Do the first item as a class. Play the audio several times.

Audioscript: Track 91

Narrator: 1

Speaker: This is my chair.

Narrator: 2

Speaker: I can see two computers.

Narrator: 3

Speaker: I read at school.

Narrator: 4

Speaker: This is my friend. She is a girl. Her name is Tina.

Narrator: 5

Girl: Hello, my name is Amy.

Girl: Hi. My name is Leah.

Girl: I like your lunchbox!

Girl: Thank you.

Narrator: 6

Speaker: Hello. What's your name?

Boy: Tom.

Speaker: Can you spell that please?

Boy: *T-O-M*

Answers
1 c   2 b   3 a   4 a   5 a   6 b

Read and write
- For items 7 and 8, demonstrate how to chant the alphabet and fill in the first missing letter of the task.

Answers
7 C, E, F   8 a, d, f   9 Ben
10 *Learner's name, beginning with a capital letter*

2 Family time

Unit overview

In this unit learners will:

- Describe their family and talk about what they do together
- Describe their family's eating habits
- Learn about eating habits in other countries
- Count from one to ten and ask simple questions about numbers: *How many … are there?*
- Understand a recipe and write one
- Ask each other simple questions about food: *Do you like …?*

Learners will build communication and literacy skills as they describe their families and compare them to other families, talk about their family's free-time activities and eating habits, make a card for a family member, read a recipe and write their own, understand what rhyme is, recite a poem, sing a song about numbers and play counting games, create a class graph and answer a questionnaire.

At the end of the unit, they will apply and personalise what they have learned by working in small groups to complete a project of their choice: making a class chart, learning a poem and teaching it to the class or making a counting book.

Language focus

Simple present tense, positive statements: *My mother reads books.*

Yes / No questions: *Does your father watch TV? Do you like (porridge)?*

Wh- questions: *What do you eat for breakfast?*

How many questions: *How many (chairs) are there?*

Imperatives: *Cut the fruit, Wash the fruit.*

Vocabulary topics: Family members, food, fruit, numbers 1–10, free-time activities, verbs, verb phrases

Critical thinking
- Understanding what rhyming words are
- Organising information into charts
- Comparing themselves to other children, assessing similarities and differences
- Understanding a questionnaire.

Self-assessment
- I can talk about families.
- I can read and write numbers up to ten.
- I can ask and answer questions about food.
- I can read and write words with the short **a** sound.

Teaching tips

Study skills: If learners have difficulty remembering the meaning or spelling of a word, tell them to look at the lesson they are working on or at previous lessons for information. Explain that their book is a resource for learning, the place where they will find the help they need.

Review the learners' work on the quiz, noting areas where they demonstrate strength and areas where they need additional instruction and practice. Use this information to customise your teaching as you continue to **Unit 3**.

Lesson 1: Think about it

What do families do together?
Learner's Book pages: 24–25
Activity Book pages: 16–17

Lesson objectives
Listening: Listen to a poem and a conversation, listen for information.

Speaking: Ask and answer questions about the family, practise theme vocabulary.

Reading: Recite and read a poem, read labels, find synonyms.

Writing: Write a message on a card.

Critical thinking: Revise the difference between a poem and a story, understand what a synonym is, make inferences.

Language focus: Present simple questions: *Do you...?*
Yes, I do / No, I don't.

Vocabulary: Family words: *mother, mum, father, dad, brother, sister, grandpa, grandma;* activities: *read books, watch TV, sing, play games, make cakes, talk*

Materials: Card, markers or coloured pencils, scissors, magazine photos of families, A4 sheets of paper.

Learner's Book

Warm up
* Revise the alphabet. Learners point to the letters as they join in the Alphabet chant (see Starter unit).
* **Is your family big or small?** Talk about the different families shown in your photos. Ask: *Are they all the same? How are they different?* Elicit answers from the class.
* If appropriate, show photos of your family. Say: *Look, my family is big / small.*
* Tell the class about things you do with your family. Show photos if appropriate, or magazine pictures, to illustrate the activities.
* Ask learners what they do with their families.

1 Read and listen 14
* Focus on the picture and identify all the family members. Say: *Look at the family. This is Sam, this is his mother ...* Repeat and ask learners to repeat the words after you.
* Point to the poem. Say: *Read and listen.* Play the audio a few times. Pause for learners to repeat each line and point to the people in the picture.
* Practise reciting the poem together. Point to the family members in the picture.

2 Sam and his family 15
* Point to the picture. Play the audio a few times. Point to the family members in turn.
* Pause after each exchange. Learners repeat and point to the corresponding people in the picture.

> **Answers**
> * Sam and his grandpa play games.
> * His grandma makes cakes.
> * His mother and baby brother read books.
> * His father often works far away, so his sister talks to Dad on the computer.

3 Topic vocabulary 16
* Direct learners' attention to the words on page 25. Play the audio and show pictures to make the meanings clear.
* Play the audio again and pause after each word. Learners point to each family member and repeat.
* Write the words on the board. Read the words together. Check for correct pronunciation.
* Tell learners to look at the picture on page 24 again. They are going to listen to Sam and decide if what he says is true or not.
* Play the audio at least twice to familiarise learners with the content. Play again and stop after each sentence to give the class time to think and decide.
* Ask learners to look at the spelling of the words on the list and find those that have a **th** sound in the middle. Elicit the correct pronunciation.

- **Critical thinking:** Explain to the class what rhyme is, i.e. words that have a similar sound. Ask them to think of rhyming words they know in English, e.g. *ten, pen, small, all.*
- **Critical thinking:** Synonyms: explain that there are words that mean the same in all languages. Discuss some examples in their first language.
- Ask learners to say the words again and find the words that rhyme, e.g. *mother / brother.* Then they look for the words that mean the same, e.g. *mother / mum.*

Audioscript: Track 16

Sam: mother

  mum

  father

  dad

  brother

  sister

  grandpa

  grandma

Sam: My mother reads books with my brother.

  My father is at home.

  I have a baby brother.

  I have three sisters.

  My sister is making a card for Grandpa.

Answers

My mother reads books with my brother. **Yes**
My father is at home. **No**
I have a baby brother. **Yes**
I have three sisters. **No**
My sister is making a card for Grandpa. **No**

mother
father
brother

Mother and *brother* rhyme.
Words that mean the same: *mum / mother; father / dad.*

 For further practice, see Activities 1 and 2 in the Activity Book.

4 Do you … ?

- Point to the pictures and say the words. Ask learners to mime the actions and repeat.
- Ask individual learners: *Do you (read books) with your family?* Help them answer: *Yes, I do. / No, I don't.*
- In pairs, learners ask and answer questions about their families.

Answers
Learners' own answers.

---

5   Make a card!

- Give out the materials for making the card. Direct learners' attention to the model in the book. You may wish to elicit from learners what they would like to say in their cards and write these phrases on the board for them to copy.
- They choose who they are making the card for. They copy the text and decorate their card.

Answers
Learners' own answers.

For further practice, see Activities 3 and 4 in the Activity Book.

Wrap up

- If appropriate, learners bring photos of their family to the class. Otherwise, they choose a magazine photograph and pretend it is their family. They show it to the class and say who each person in the picture is.

Activity Book

1 Girls and boys

- Learners look at the **Word box** and say the words.
- Point to the icons and ask: *Is your sister a boy or girl?* Learners answer and write the word in the correct column. Ask about other members of the family.
- **Critical thinking:** Ask learners to justify their choices.

Answers

father	*mother*
brother	*sister*
grandpa	*grandma*

(Learners' own answer for *me*.)

---

2 Your family

- Give learners pencils and crayons and a sheet of paper. They draw their family and label the family members.
- When they have finished they describe their family to the class.
- They answer the question. They can compare whose family is the biggest.

Answers
Learners' own answers.

---

3 This is for you!

- Read through the instructions. Then ask learners to read each sentence in turn with a partner.
- Do the example as a class. Ask: *Who is it for? Your father? Mother?* Provide help as needed.

- Learners look at the pictures and decide on their answers.
- When they have finished, check as a class and ask learners to justify their choice.
- **Critical thinking:** Learners learn to make inferences from the visual information they have in the pictures. This information will help them decide whose present each is.

> **Answers**
> **1d** *sister*
> **2b** *mother*
> **3c** *baby brother*
> **4a** *father (given as example)*

Challenge

- Read the instructions. Learners circle the words. You may wish to check as a class.

> **Answers**
> (This) is for my (father)
> (This) is for my (mother)
> (This) is for my baby (brother)
> (This) is for my sister.

4 Make a card

- Tell learners to make this card for a different family member. They can then take the cards home as a gift.

I can talk about families.

- Direct learners' attention to the self-evaluation question at the top of page 16. Ask them to think and answer. Emphasise the importance of giving an honest answer.

> **Answers**
> Learners' own answers.

Differentiated instruction

Additional support and practice

- Play a game. Point to the different family members in a magazine picture or in the book and say the name (*mother, grandpa*, etc.). Make some mistakes. Learners say: *yes* or *no*, and if they say *no*, they say the correct word.

Extend and challenge

- 🗨 Give each pair a sheet of paper. They create a 'fictional family', e.g. aliens, animals or people. They label the family members and give them names.

Lesson 2: Find out more

Breakfast time

Learner's Book pages: 26–27
Activity Book pages: 18–19

Lesson objectives

Listening: Listen and respond to informational text.

Speaking: Ask and answer questions about eating habits and preferences, practise topic vocabulary.

Reading: Read informational text, read and discuss a chart.

Writing: Complete sentences about yourself and others, write a recipe, make a chart.

Critical thinking: Learners compare themselves to other children, establishing similarities and differences, and make a chart.

Language focus: Positive statements: *I eat (bread), She / He eats (rice)*; imperatives: *cut, wash, eat*; questions: *What do you eat for breakfast? I eat …*

Vocabulary: Breakfast foods: *bread, rice, beans, noodles, soup, eggs, cereal with milk, yogurt*; fruit: *apple, banana, grapes, mango, orange, pear, strawberry, pineapple, watermelon*

Materials: Word cards with small pictures on them: *bread, rice, beans, noodles, soup, eggs, cereal with milk, fruit, yogurt*; sheets of paper; crayons or coloured pencils; old magazines; glue; scissors; map of the world.

Learner's Book

☞ Warm up

- Recite the family poem in **Lesson 1** and review the names of family members: Point to the brother. *Who's this?*

☞ Introduce vocabulary

- Introduce *bread, rice, beans, noodles, soup, eggs, cereal with milk, fruit, yogurt* using the word cards.
- Show the card and say the word. Learners repeat.

Guess the word

- Begin drawing an item of food very slowly on the whiteboard. Learners guess what it is.

1 Before you read 🔊17

- Open books at page 26. Point to each photo. Say, *this is John. Look at his breakfast. What does he have for breakfast?* Learners answer. Repeat with Trang.
- Play the audio. Point to the pictures in turn. Play the audio again, pausing to allow children to repeat each line. Learners follow in their book.

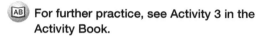

Audioscript: Track 17

Speaker 1: John lives in the United States. He eats pancakes for breakfast.

Speaker 2: Trang lives in Vietnam. She eats noodles for breakfast.

> **Answers**
> John eats pancakes.
> Trang eats noodles.

2 What do you eat for breakfast?

- Point to the vocabulary pictures and say: *I eat (fruit and cereal with milk). And you, what do you eat for breakfast?* Learners respond.
- In pairs, learners ask and answer about their breakfast habits.

> **Suggested answers**
> I eat cereal with milk.
> He / she eats eggs.

3 Write

- Direct learners' attention to the writing activity. Model the answer with one of the learners. Write their answer on the board.
- Ask learners to complete the sentences about themselves and their partner.

> **Answers**
> Learners' own answers.

[AB] For further practice, see Activities 1 and 2 in the Activity Book.

4 Talia and Jacob's fruit salad 18

- Use the pictures at the side of page 27 to introduce the new vocabulary. Point to each picture and say the word. Learners repeat. Check for correct pronunciation.
- Say and mime: *I like (mango and strawberries). Yummy! Look! Which fruits do you like?* Help learners answer.
- Ask: *Do you like fruit salad? Look, Talia and Jacob like fruit salad. This is their recipe. Let's listen.*
- Play the recording a few times. Mime the actions. Learners follow in their books and mime after you.

Audioscript: Track 18

Jacob: My sister and I eat fruit salad for breakfast. This is our recipe.

1 mango

10 grapes

1 banana

4 strawberries

Wash the fruit.

Cut up the fruit.

Eat your fruit salad.

5 Write a recipe

- Ask learners to look at the fruits on page 27 and choose the ones they like for their fruit salad.
- Ask learners to write a recipe in their notebooks using the fruits they like.

[AB] For further practice, see Activity 3 in the Activity Book.

6 A class chart

- Draw attention to the chart. Read the title of the chart and the answer in the first row. Ask the class: *How many children like bananas? Let's count.* Repeat these steps with the next row.
- **Make your own class chart:** Give learners sheets of paper. They copy the chart on the paper. They choose a fruit and write the title question, then they circulate asking the question.
- Ask questions about the learners' completed charts: *How many children like apples?*
- **Critical thinking:** Draw learners' attention to how the chart is organised and how to work with it.
- **Home–school link:** Learners ask parents what their favourite breakfast was when they were children. They draw a picture and bring it to class, and describe it to a partner.

Wrap up

- Write the title *Our class breakfast* on a large piece of paper and ask learners to suggest what words to include. Write the words the children say on the piece of paper.

Activity Book

1 What do you eat for breakfast?

- Learners find the missing words in the **Word box** and write the sentences. Circulate and give help as necessary with writing.
- **Critical thinking:** Ask learners to compare what they eat with what the children in the pictures eat. How similar or different is their breakfast? Would they like to eat the same things?

> **Answers**
> 1 I eat soup.
> 2 My sister eats noodles.
> 3 My dad eats eggs.
> 4 My mum eats yogurt.

2 Do you like it?

- Direct learners' attention to the questions and answers. Read the questions and encourage them to answer orally first. Then they circle the correct option.
- For the second part, tell them to copy the answer that is true for them.

> **Answers**
> Learners' own answers.

3 Write a recipe

- Learners write their own recipe using the model in the book. They can decorate the recipe with pictures of the fruits in their salad.

> **Answers**
> Learners' own answers.

Challenge

- Read the instructions. Learners write the words. You may wish to check as a class.

> **Suggested answers**
> Red fruits: *strawberry, watermelon*
> Yellow fruits: *banana, pineapple*
> Green fruits: *apple*

I can ask and answer questions about food.

- Direct learners' attention to the self-evaluation question at the top of page 18. Ask them to think and answer. Emphasise the importance of giving an honest answer.

> **Answers**
> Learners' own answers.

Differentiated instruction

Additional support and practice

- Ask learners to go through old magazines and cut out items of food they have learned. They glue them on sheets of paper and copy the food words. They show their food pictures to the class and say the word.

Extend and challenge

- In their journals, learners write what their family likes to eat for breakfast using vocabulary from **Lessons 1** and **2**.
- Read the captions under the photos of the children on page 26. Are either of the children from the country you are in? Are either from a nearby country? Help learners locate the two countries on a map or globe. Trace the route from their country to each of these other countries. Encourage them to say, e.g. *John lives in the United States. I live in (name of country).*

Lesson 3: Letters and sounds

Short a
Learner's Book pages: 28–29
Activity Book pages: 20–21

Lesson objectives

Listening: Listen to a rhyme and a story, identify the sound of short **a**.

Speaking: Say a rhyme, sing a spelling song, make a new song.

Reading: Recognise words with short **a**, identify words that rhyme, read a story.

Critical thinking: Finding rhyming words.

Language focus: Blending short **a** words, rhyming

Vocabulary: *cat, hat, lap, map, nap, cap, clap, back, glasses*

Materials: Real objects to represent the vocabulary above if possible, otherwise pictures of a hat, a pair of glasses, a toy cat, a cap; paper and pencils, crayons, A4 sheets of paper.

Learner's Book

☞ Warm up

- Play *Mum says* or *Dad says*, a variation of *Simon says*, to revise actions from **Lessons 1** and **2**. Say: *Mum says wash the apple. Mum says read a book. Mum says fly a kite.* etc.
- **Critical thinking:** Remind the class of the difference between a poem and a story, and the concept of rhyme discussed in **Lesson 1**.
- Ask learners to look for rhymes in the previous lessons, e.g. **Unit 1 Lesson 1, Unit 2 Lesson 1**.
- Read the rhymes together. Ask them to identify and circle the words that rhyme.
- Pick up the toy cat (or picture of a cat) and ask: *What is it?* Elicit: *A cat.*
- Show the hat (or picture of a hat) and say: *Look, a hat. A cat and a hat.* Do the same with the cap and the glasses. Ask learners to repeat the words after you.

1 Listen and look 19

- Learners open books at page 28. Point to the pictures and say: *Let's listen.*
- Play the audio and point to letter **a** and the pictures in turn.
- Play the audio again. Learners repeat.

> **Audioscript:** Track 19
> **Speaker:** a
>   apple
>   cat

2 Grandma's glasses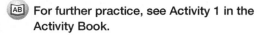

- Tell the class they are going to listen to a rhyme. Play the audio. Mime the actions to help learners understand *folds her hands / puts them on her lap*.
- Play the rhyme again. Pause after each line for learners to repeat.
- As learners grow more confident, invite them to say the rhyme without help. Begin by saying the first words of each line and ask them to finish, e.g. *Here are Grandma's ... , Here is Grandma's ... .* Progressively, say fewer words until learners are able to say complete lines by themselves. Check for correct pronunciation as you go through the rhyme.

> **Audioscript:** Track 20
> **Speaker:** Here are Grandma's glasses.
>
> Here is Grandma's hat.
>
> This is how she folds her hands
>
> And puts them on her lap.

3 Rhyming words

- Draw attention to the words. Say the words and ask learners to repeat them.
- Ask them to find the similarities in the words: *They all contain the sound **a** and they all finish with **p**.* Then ask what the differences are: *They begin with a different letter*.
- Ask learners to spell the three words: *map, lap* and *nap*.
- Turn to the next pictures (*cap* and *clap*). Point and ask: *What's this? Can you spell it?* Encourage learners to answer. Then they write the words: *cap* and *clap*.

AB For further practice, see Activity 1 in the Activity Book.

4 Phonics story 21

- Direct learners' attention to the pictures. Tell learners that you are going to listen to a story about a cat.
- Play the recording once and point at each picture in turn. Play the recording again and mime to make the meaning of *back* clear to learners.
- Play the recording again. Invite learners to repeat after each line.
- Ask learners to count the words that they hear with the short **a**.

> **Audioscript:** Track 21
> **Speaker: *The cat***
>
> The cat has a hat.
>
> The cat has a map.
>
> The cat claps.
>
> The cat is back.
>
> The cat has a nap in Dad's lap.

> **Answers**
> There are eight words with the short **a** sound: *cat, hat, map, claps, back, nap, Dad* and *lap*.

AB For further practice, see Activities 2 and 3 in the Activity Book.

Wrap up

- **Portfolio opportunity:** Pass out paper and pencils. Learners write their name at the top of the paper, then write words they remember that contain the short **a**. They can also draw the corresponding pictures. Collect the learners' work, write the date on the back, and save in the learners' portfolio.

Activity Book

1 Read and draw

- Read the sentences as a class. Point to the pictures and ask: *Where is Dad's hat?* Ask learners to complete and colour each picture.

2 Short *a* sound

- Ask learners to look at the first pair of pictures. Say the words. Point at the first word and ask: *Does this word have the short **a**?*
- Learners say *yes* or *no* and circle the words accordingly. Continue with the other words, reading them aloud to learners so they have a model.

> **Answers**
> The words with short **a** sounds are: *hand, stand, cat, clap, dad, apple*

3 Write the words

- Model the first word on the board. Invite learners to work on the others independently. Circulate to help if necessary.

> **Answers**
> clap   hand   cat

I can read and write words with the short *a* sound.

- Direct learners' attention to the self-evaluation question at the top of page 20. Ask them to think and answer. Emphasise the importance of giving an honest answer.

> **Answers**
> Learners' own answers.

Differentiated instruction

Additional support and practice

- See letter and sound activities suggested in the Starter unit (page 19).

Extend and challenge

- Give learners spelling dictation, for example: C-A-P. Can they identify the word they have written?

Lesson 4: Use of English

Let's count!

Learner's Book pages: 30–31
Activity Book pages: 22–23

Lesson objectives

Listening: Listen and sing a song about numbers, follow instructions.

Speaking: Count from one to ten, ask and answer questions about numbers, do simple sums and subtractions.

Reading: Read the numbers one to ten forwards and backwards.

Writing: Write the numbers one to ten.

Language focus: *How many ... are there?, there is ... / there are ...*

Vocabulary: Numbers one to ten, colours (review), *door, window, bed,* numbers

Materials: Crayons, pencils or markers of different colours; two or three pictures of houses. For each learner: ten index cards, a paper clip, a pencil and one large circle of card (diameter at least 11 cm) divided into six equal segments. Each segment contains one of the following artworks: two beds, a TV, seven pencils, a table, five bowls, four spoons. Small cards numbered 1–10 and a small bag to play bingo, a sheet of A4 paper for each learner, a copy of **Photocopiable activity 3** for each learner.

Learner's Book

☞ Warm up

- Sit in a circle. Display photos of families and food items the class has learned. Divide the class into two or three groups, depending on the number of learners, and have a spelling competition.

- Show a picture and ask a group to say the word and then spell it. The group gets a point if it knows the word and spells it correctly. After a period of time, the winning group is the one which has the most points.
- Sit in a circle. Place the crayons or markers in the middle of the circle. Say: *Find the (blue crayons). Let's count the crayons. How many blue crayons are there?*
- Learners count and answer, e.g. *Five.* Echo their answer: *Yes, there are (five) crayons.* Continue with more examples.

1 ⬛ How many?

- Learners open books at page 30. Direct their attention to the picture: *Look at this house. Look at the door. Look at the windows. Let's count!*
- Point to the first question. Read it aloud and invite learners to answer. Then, point at the answer on the page and say: *Yes! There is one door.* Repeat with the second question.
- Ask learners how many doors and windows there are in their houses. Allow time for them to think about their answer and then invite the more confident ones to speak first.

> **Answers**
> Learner's own answers.

2 🗨 Play a counting game

- Give learners a circle of card, a paper clip and a pencil each. Explain and model how to make the spinner. In pairs learners take turns to ask and answer questions depending on where the spinner lands. Q: *How many beds are there?* A: *There are two beds.*
- Write the questions on the board. Practise saying the questions.

3 📝 ⬛ 🎵 Sing a counting song 22

- Give each learner ten index cards, crayons or markers. Ask them to write the figures 1 to 10, one on each card, as illustrated in the Learner's Book on page 31.
- Call out numbers and ask learners to hold up the corresponding number card.
- Direct learners' attention to the number cards on page 31. Ask them to count aloud. Then ask them to count backwards. Repeat this a few times at a progressively quicker pace.
- Draw learners' attention to the song. Tell learners to put their number cards in order on their tables and point at them in turn as they listen.
- Play the song once, miming as necessary to make the meaning clear to the learners.
- Play the song again. Learners put up the corresponding number as they hear it and mime along.
- Progressively encourage them to sing along as you continue singing the verses until you get to 1. At this point sing the last line provided in the Learner's Book: *And the little one says, 'Good Night!'*

Audioscript: Track 22

Speaker: *10 in the bed*

There are 10 in the bed

And the little one says,

'Roll over. Roll over.'

So they all roll over and 1 falls out.

There are 9 in the bed

And the little one says,

'Roll over. Roll over.'

So they all roll over and 1 falls out.

…

There is 1 in the bed

And the little one says, 'Good night!'

 For further practice, see Activities 1, 2 and 3 in the Activity Book.

Wrap up

- Play bingo. Before the lesson, write the numbers one to ten on pieces of paper and put them in a bag.
- Draw a 2 × 3 grid on the board. Ask learners to copy it on a sheet of paper and write six different numbers, one in each square.
- Play bingo in the usual way.

Activity Book

1 How many?

- Focus on the pictures. Ask learners to count the items in turn. Ask: *How many (doors) are there?*
- Learners answer as a class, then write the answers.

Answers
1 There
2 There is **1** door.
3 There are **2** windows.
4 There are **6** chairs.

2 Add numbers

- Review the numbers and do the first sum as a class.
- Divide the class into pairs and ask learners to do the rest of the sums. Circulate, helping as necessary. Check as a class.

Answers
$2 + 2 = 4$
*Two and two is **four**.*
$3 + 2 = 5$
*Three and two is **five**.*

3 Take away numbers

- Explain **Activity 3**. Do the first subtraction sum as a class.
- In pairs, invite the class to do the rest of the sums. Circulate helping as necessary. Check as a class.

Answers
$7 - 2 = \textbf{5}$
$5 - 2 = \textbf{3}$
$3 - 2 = \textbf{1}$
*There is **1** in the bed.*

I can read and write numbers up to 10.

- Direct learners' attention to the self-evaluation question. Ask them to think and answer. Emphasise the importance of giving an honest answer.

Answers
Learners' own answers.

Differentiated instruction

Additional support and practice

- Do **Photocopiable activity 3** as a class as extension and revision work.

Extend and challenge

- Ask individual learners to prepare sums and subtractions, two of each, and pass them to another learner. They then solve their partner's sums.

Lesson 5: Read and respond

Learner's Book pages: 32–35
Activity Book pages: 24–25

Lesson objectives

Listening: Listen to a story.

Speaking: Make predictions about a non-fiction text, talk about the text, discuss family roles.

Reading: Read along as you listen to a non-fiction text, answer a questionnaire, practise sight words.

Writing: Write words in speech bubbles to complete a conversation, answer a questionnaire, write about own family.

Writing tip: Use a capital letter at the beginning of a sentence and a full stop at the end of a sentence. Use **and**.

Critical thinking: Predicting content from pictures, understanding the difference between fiction and non-fiction, understanding what a questionnaire is for and how to ask and answer the questions in it.

Language focus: *This dad works on the computer. This mum cooks dinner.*

Vocabulary: Family words (revision); *grown-ups, children, people, little (brother / sister);* activities: *work on the computer, cook dinner, work, lay the table, tidy (her) room, play together, talk, have fun, laugh, help each other, do homework*

Materials: Pictures of families in different situations (from **Lesson 1**) or, if appropriate, photos of your family and the learners'; illustrated word cards for the new vocabulary; paper and pencils, crayons, A4 sheets of paper.

Learner's Book

👉 Warm up

- Show pictures of families or, if appropriate, a photo of your family, and review family vocabulary. Learners then show photos of their own families or magazine pictures and talk about family members.
- Remind the class about Sam's family and the things they do together on Saturday evening (Lesson 1). Review the vocabulary from Lesson 1.

👉 Introduce vocabulary

- Use the photos or pictures to introduce *grown-ups, people* and *children*. Ask questions: *How many people are there in this photo / classroom? How many grown-ups? How many children?*
- Show the illustrated word cards and mime to introduce the actions: *work on the computer, cook dinner, work, lay the table, tidy (her) room, play together, talk, have fun, laugh.*
- Learners repeat and mime the actions.
- Play a game of *Mum says* or *Dad says* using the new vocabulary.

1 Before you read 23

- Open books at page 32. Read the title of the text. Learners look at the pictures on pages 32 to 34 and predict what the text will be about.
- **Critical thinking:** Explain that they can use pictures to have an idea of what a text will be about and in this way understand it more easily.
- Point to the pictures and revise the new vocabulary. Ask: *What does the father / mother do?*
- Play the audio. Point to the pictures in turn.
- Play the audio again, pausing to allow learners to repeat each line. Mime *little* with your hands.
- Focus on the last picture on page 34. Remind learners of the importance of being polite and saying *Please* and *Thank you.*
- Invite individuals or pairs of learners to read the words. Ask more confident learners to dramatise the text.

Audioscript: Track 23

Families work and have fun
In a family there are grown-ups and children.
This family is small. This family is big.

The grown-ups work.
This mum cooks the dinner.
This dad works on the computer.

The children work.
This boy lays the table.
This girl tidies her room.

Families have fun together.
These children play together.
These men talk and laugh together.

People in a family help each other.
This boy helps his little sister.
'Thank you,' says the girl.

This girl helps her little brother.
'Thank you,' says the boy.

---

2 💬 Family questionnaire

- Direct learners' attention to the questionnaire on page 35. Read the questions through together.
- **Critical thinking:** Ask the class what questionnaires are used for. Focus on the number of questions, categories and number of answers. Explain the meaning of the word *sometimes*.
- Ask them what they can use a questionnaire for at school, e.g. *Find out what children like to study / do in their free time.*
- Divide the class into pairs. Explain the activity. Learners ask each other the questions and write the answers in their notebooks.
- When they have finished, ask individual learners to report their answers to the class. Ask: *How many people are there in (Amira's) family?* Help learners answer in a complete sentence: *There are (four) people in (her) family.*

Answers
Learners' own answers.

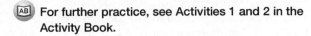 For further practice, see Activities 1 and 2 in the Activity Book.

3 📝 Draw and write

- Discuss with learners how they help at home. Elicit examples and provide additional vocabulary as necessary.

Writing tip

- Focus on the example sentence. Remind learners of what capital letters are. Ask: *Are there capital letters in this sentence?* Explain the use of a capital letter at the beginning of a sentence.
- Explain what a full stop is and when to use it.

Words to remember

- Write the words *this, his* and *her* on the board.
- Learners look for the sight words in the **Activity 1** text. How many times do they see the word? Have them count on their fingers.

Answers
this appears eight times
his appears once
her appears twice

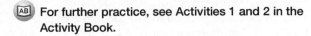 For further practice, see Activity 3 in the Activity Book.

👉 Wrap up

- Ask learners what job they like doing most at home and what job they like doing the least. Elicit answers, e.g. *I like washing the dishes. I don't like tidying my room.* Write the choices on the board to see which the most and least popular jobs are.

Activity Book

1 Your family

- Draw learners' attention to **Activity 1**. Read the questions together and ask learners to say the answers before writing.
- Focus on the example in the **Writing tip**. Explain that we use **and** when we speak about more than one member of the family, e.g. *my father **and** my mother*.
- **Informal assessment opportunity:** Circulate as learners work. Informally assess their receptive and productive language skills. Ask questions. You may want to take notes on their responses.

Writing tip

Focus on the examples. Explain that they use **and** when they speak about more than one member of the family, e.g. *my father **and** my mother*.

> **Answers**
> Learners' own answers.

2 Helping

- Turn to **Activity 2**. Discuss polite forms *Please, Thank you.*
- Act out situations in which you would use these. Turn to the activity and help learners complete the missing expression.

> **Answer**
> Thank you.

3 Draw and write

- Ask learners to draw a picture of how they help at home, then write a sentence about it.

Challenge

- Ask them what they would say in that situation. Help them write a speech bubble for their picture.

> **Answers**
> Learners' own answers.

I can talk about families.

Direct learners' attention to the self-evaluation question at the top of page 24. Ask them to think and answer. Emphasise the importance of giving an honest answer.

> **Answers**
> Learners' own answers.

Differentiated instruction

Additional support and practice

- Give TPR instructions to revise the action verbs in this unit.
- Play a guessing game to revise food vocabulary. Begin drawing an item of food on the board. Learners guess the word.

Extend and challenge

- 🗣 Pairs of learners open their books at the School section of the **Picture dictionary** (page 137). They point to and say the words they know.
- **Early literacy:** Write a few words from the unit on the board omitting some letters, e.g. vowels. Ask learners to supply the missing letters and spell the words.

Lesson 6: Choose a project

What do families do together?

Learner's Book pages: 36–37
Activity Book pages: 26–27

Lesson objectives

Listening: Listen to and follow directions, listen to comprehension items in the Activity Book quiz.

Speaking: Present your project to the class.

Reading: Make a chart, learn a poem, make a counting book, read sentences to do a matching exercise in the Activity Book quiz.

Writing: Fill in a chart, write words in a counting book, write name and letters in the Activity Book quiz.

Language focus: Unit 2 Review

Materials:

A Make a chart: One copy of **Photocopiable activity 4** for each learner; pens or pencils.

B Learn a poem: Card and drawing supplies.

C Make a counting book: Writing / drawing supplies; sheets of paper or card to make the book; number cards; camera (optional); printer (optional).

Learner's Book

➩ Warm up

- Play a guessing game to revise TPR directions: *work on the computer, cook dinner, work, lay the table, tidy (her) room, play together, talk, have fun, laugh, help each other, do homework, read books, watch TV, sing, play games, make cakes, talk.*

- Divide the class into two groups. Each group takes turns to give an order to the other group. The other group then mimes the action.

Choose a project

- Learners choose an end-of-unit project to work on. Look at the learner-made samples and help individuals choose. Move the children into groups depending on their choices. Provide materials.
- **Portfolio opportunity:** If possible, leave the learner projects on display for a short while, then consider filing the projects, photos or scans of the work, in learners' portfolios. Write the date on the work.

A Make a chart

- Read the directions in the Learner's Book and give each learner a copy of **Photocopiable activity 4**. Each learner chooses a word from the unit and writes it in their chart.
- They circulate, asking the question. Then they report back to the class.

B Learn a poem

- Read the directions. Read and practise the poem together. Learners may also draw pictures to go with their poem.
- In groups they teach the poem to other learners.

C Make a counting book

- Read the directions. Learners decide what objects and how many of each to include in the book.
- They draw or take photos and write the words under each, e.g. *3 apples.*

Look what I can do!

- Review the *I can ...* statements. Learners demonstrate what they can do.

Activity Book

Unit 2 Quiz: Look what I can do!

Listen 92 [CD2 Track 39]

- For items 1 to 6, learners listen and tick the correct picture. Do the first item as a class. Play the audio several times.

Audioscript: Track 92

Narrator: 1

Speaker: This is my mother. I call her Mum.

Narrator: 2

Speaker: Who is that for?

Boy: It's for my father. It's his birthday.

Narrator: 3

Speaker: Do you like soup?

Boy: Yes, I do. I like soup!

Narrator: 4

Speaker: There are six beds.

Narrator: 5

Speaker 1: How many windows are there?

Speaker 2: There are two windows.

Speaker 1: How many doors?

Speaker 2: There is one door.

Speaker 1: Two windows and one door.

Speaker 2: Yes! Can you see it?

Speaker 1: Yes, I can!

Narrator: 6

Speaker: The boy helps his little sister. His little sister says, "Thank you!"

Answers					
1 c	2 b	3 b	4 a	5 b	6 a

Read and write

- For items 7 to 8, learners match the words to the pictures. Demonstrate by tracing with your finger. For items 9 to 10, learners write the words to go with the pictures.

Answers			
7 a	8 b	9 *cat*	10 *dad*

3 Fun and games

Unit overview

In this unit learners will:
- Understand, follow and give instructions
- Create a game
- Compare and contrast games
- Ask each other simple questions.

Learners will build communication and literacy skills as they describe games they play and compare them to other games, learn about games played in other countries, write instructions for a game they have created, read and act out a story, understand the basic conventions of a play, assess the characters in a play, fill in a chart, and classify words according to a sound.

At the end of the unit, they will apply and personalise what they have learned by working in small groups to complete a project of their choice: making a game for the class, making a body parts poster or making up a clapping game.

Language focus

Can for ability

Questions: *Can you ...? Yes, I can. No, I can't.*

Positive statements: *I can run like a puppy.*

Imperative: *(Throw) the ball.*

Prepositions: *on, under, next to*

Vocabulary topics: Verbs, verb phrases, parts of the body, parts of a room, classroom furniture, animals

Critical thinking

- Problem-solving: creating a game
- Understanding the rules of a game
- Comparing, assessing similarities and differences
- Working with charts
- Understanding what a play is
- Classifying.

Self-assessment

- I can talk about ways to have fun.
- I can ask and answer questions: *Can you ...?*
- I can say where things are.
- I can name parts of the body.
- I can read and write words with the short **u** sound.

Teaching tips

Values: Teach polite game-playing 'good sport' phrases, e.g. *You won! I won. Good game. Let's play again. It's your turn. Good luck!* Discuss with learners the importance of fair play and not cheating.

Review the learners' work on the Activity Book quiz, noting areas where they demonstrate strength and areas where they need additional instruction and practice. Use this information to customise your teaching as you continue to **Unit 4**.

Lesson 1: Think about it

What games can we play?
Learner's Book pages: 38–39

Activity Book pages: 28–29

Lesson objectives

Listening: Listen to a poem and a conversation, listen for information.

Speaking: Ask and answer questions about games, practise theme vocabulary, spell words.

Reading: Recite and read a poem, read labels, find synonyms.

Writing: Write instructions for a game.

Critical thinking: Problem-solving, creating a game.

Language focus: Imperatives: *Bounce the ball, Roll it*

Vocabulary: *throw, catch, roll, hit, kick, bounce, ball, box, bat*

Materials: A small rubber ball for each learner, boxes and balls of different sizes, markers or coloured pencils, magazine photos of children playing games, A4 sheets of paper.

Learner's Book

Warm up

- Play a game of *Simon says* to revise the verbs learned in **Unit 2**.
- **What games can we play?** Talk about games you played when you were a child. Ask learners about games they play. Ask: *Are they the same? How are they different?* Elicit answers from the class. Show photos of children playing games, especially ball games. Ask: *What's the name of this game?*

Think about it

- Open books at page 38. Direct learners' attention to the instructions.
- Mime *clap* and *bounce*. Say the words and ask learners to mime and repeat after you.

1 Read and listen 24

- Point to the poem. Say: *Read and listen.* Play the audio a few times.
- Demonstrate the actions with a small rubber ball: *bounce, roll, throw, catch.*
- Pause for learners to repeat each line and mime.
- Practise reciting the poem together as you bounce the ball.

Audioscript: Track 24

Speaker: Bounce the ball

Ball, ball,

Bounce the ball!

Roll it, throw it,

Catch the ball!

---

2 Which picture? 25

- Point to the pictures. Play the audio a few times. Pause after each exchange as learners repeat and point to the corresponding people in the picture.

Audioscript: Track 25

Narrator: 1

Girl 1: Hit the ball!
Girl 2: Oops. I missed.

Narrator: 2

Girl 2: Throw the ball to Bingo, Dad!
Dad: Good dog! Bingo can catch a ball!

Narrator: 3

Boy 1: 1, 2, 3 … Roll the ball!

Narrator: 4

Girl 1: Ball, ball,
Bounce the ball.
Ball, ball,
Bounce the ball.

Narrator: 5

Boy: Hey, Mum! Watch me kick the ball!
Goal!

Answers
1d hit   **2a** throw, catch   **3c** roll   **4b** bounce   **5e** kick

---

3 Topic vocabulary 26

- Learners look at page 39. Direct their attention to the words. Play the audio and mime to make the meanings clear.
- Play the audio and pause after each word. Learners point at the correct picture and repeat.
- They listen again and mime the actions.
- Write the words on the board. Read the words together. Check for correct pronunciation.

- Learners look at the picture on page 38 again. They listen and decide what word is spelt.
- Play the recording through at least twice. Play again but pause after each word to give the class time to think and decide.
- **Study skills:** Remind learners to look in their books for the new words and copy from there if they have difficulty remembering them.

Audioscript: Track 26
Speaker: Throw
Girl: Throw the ball to Bingo, Dad!
Speaker: Catch
Dad: Bingo can catch a ball!
Speaker: Roll
Boy: 1, 2, 3, Roll the ball!
Speaker: Hit
Girl: Hit the ball!
Speaker: Kick
Boy: Hey mum! Watch me kick the ball!
Speaker: Bounce
Girl: Ball, ball, bounce the ball. Ball, ball, bounce the ball.
Speaker: H-I-T. [pause] H-I-T.

K-I-C-K. [pause] K-I-C-K

C-A-T-C-H. [pause] C-A-T-C-H.

B-O-U-N-C-E. [pause] B-O-U-N-C-E.

R-O-L-L. [pause] R-O-L-L.

T-H-R-O-W. [pause] T-H-R-O-W.

Answers
hit
kick
catch
bounce
roll
throw

 For further practice, see Activity 1 in the Activity Book.

4 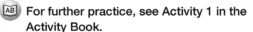 Can you do it?

- Point to the pictures and sentences and ask individual learners: *Can you kick a ball / catch a ball?* Help them answer: *Yes, I can / No, I can't.*
- Point to each picture and sentence in turn. Ask the class to mime the actions and repeat the sentences after you.
- In pairs, learners ask and answer questions about what they can do.

Answers
Learners' own answers.

 For further practice, see Activity 2 in the Activity Book.

5 Make up a game with a ball

- Give learners balls and boxes of different sizes. They can choose to roll, throw, bounce or kick the ball, using the boxes to invent their own game.

Answers
Learners' own answers.

Wrap up

- Mime the actions and ask the class to say what you are doing. After a few rounds, you can ask more confident learners to take up your role.

Activity Book

1 What can we do with a ball?

- Focus on the pictures. Ask learners to find the correct action word in the **Word box**.
- Learners write the word in the correct sentence. Check as a class.

Answers
1 Throw
2 Bounce
3 Hit
4 Catch
5 Kick
6 Roll

2 Can you do it?

- Ask the questions and allow time for learners to think and decide on their answers. Learners circle their answers for the first two questions, and write their answer for the third.
- You could check by asking them to make a show of hands and answering as a class.

Answers
Learners' own answers.

Challenge

Learners draw and write about their made-up game in the Activity Book.

- They write and draw pictures in their books.
- Ask each group to teach their game to the class.
- **Critical thinking:** This is a problem-solving activity which will require learners to make decisions together, decide on a sequence for their game, evaluate problems and use the correct language to describe the game they have created. Allow plenty of time for preparation.

Answers
Learners' own answers.

Audioscript: Track 93

Narrator: 1

Speaker: Ball, ball, bounce the ball, bounce the ball, bounce the ball.

Narrator: 2

Speaker: Catch the ball, Bingo! Good dog!

Narrator: 3

Speaker: 1, 2, 3, Go!

Speaker: Paper and rock.

Speaker: Paper can cover rock, so PAPER wins!

Speaker: Good game! Let's play again.

Narrator: 4

Speaker: I can sit on the rug.

Narrator: 5

Speaker 1: Where is the duck?

Speaker 2: It's under the table.

Speaker: 1 Where?

Speaker 2: Under the table.

Speaker 1: Oh yes. I see it.

Narrator: 6

Speaker 1: Put your pencil next to the book.

Speaker 2: Next to the book?

Speaker1: Yes, that's right. Put your pencil next to the book.

Speaker 2: OK!

Answers

1 b   2 a   3 a   4 c   5 b   6 b

Read and write

For items 7 to 8, learners match the words to the pictures. Demonstrate by tracing with your finger.
For items 9 to 10, learners write the words to go with the pictures.

Answers

7 Picture a   8 Picture a   9 sun   10 bug

4 Making things

Unit overview

In this unit learners will:

- Say and ask what they and other people are doing
- Describe what they and others are wearing or doing
- Make, and talk about making, quilts and pictures using shapes and colours
- Write a thank you letter.

Learners will build communication and literacy skills as they describe what they are wearing and doing, learn the words of a traditional song, follow a pattern to create a new song, read and act out a rhyming story, read a traditional story, discuss the plot of the story, and write a letter.

At the end of the unit, they will apply and personalise what they have learned by working in small groups to complete a project of their choice: making a fashion model, making a shape animal, or drawing a picture based on the story they have read.

Language focus

Present continuous: positive statements and *Wh*-questions: *I'm wearing a pilot's hat. What is she wearing?; Let's … ; I like …*

Vocabulary topics: clothes, colours, shapes, characters

Critical thinking

- Creating and combining patterns
- Classifying into given categories
- Understanding the concept of synonyms
- Matching questions and answers
- Understanding the basic conventions of letter writing.

Self-assessment

- I can talk about shapes.
- I can say what I am wearing.
- I can say what people are doing.
- I can read and write words with the short **e** sound.

Teaching tip

Review the learners' work on the Activity Book quiz, noting areas where they demonstrate strength and areas where they need additional instruction and practice. Use this information to customise your teaching as you continue to **Unit 5**.

Lesson 1: Think about it

What can we make with shapes?

Learner's Book pages: 52–53

Activity Book pages: 40–41

Lesson objectives

Listening: Listen to a poem, listen for information.

Speaking: Ask and answer questions about what people are wearing, practise theme vocabulary.

Reading: Recite and read a poem, read labels.

Writing: Write about what you are wearing.

Writing tip: Contracted form *I'm*.

Language focus: Present continuous: *I'm wearing a pilot's hat. What is she wearing?*

Vocabulary: Clothes: *dress, shirt, trousers, jacket, skirt, shoes, top, hat*; characters: *clown, king, princess, superhero, pilot; plane, cook, funny, frown, silver, gold, ring, party*

Materials: Pictures of the vocabulary items above, or old items of clothing for the clothes vocabulary, markers or coloured pencils, magazine photos, scissors, glue, a large sheet of paper, file cards, a dice.

Learner's Book

☞ Warm up

- Revise vocabulary from previous units. Distribute vocabulary cards around the room and play *I spy …*
- Illustrate the word *shapes* by drawing a circle, triangle, square, etc. on the board.
- Remind learners of the colours they know. Show pictures of patterns with different shapes in them and ask learners to say the shapes they see.

Think about it

- Show pictures to introduce *clown, king, a silver ring.* Mime *funny* and *frown* or show pictures to illustrate the meaning of the words.
- Ask learners to mime and repeat the words after you.

1 Read and listen 35

- Open books at page 52. Focus on the picture. Ask: *Can you see a clown? A king? Who else can you see in the picture? What are they doing?*
- Point to the poem. Say: *Read and listen.* Play the audio a few times.
- Pause for learners to repeat each line and mime.
- Practise reciting the poem together.

Audioscript: Track 35

See Learner's Book page 52.

Answers

There is a clown and a king in the poem and in the picture.

☞ Introduce new vocabulary

- Show pictures of words *pilot, princess, party, superhero* and *cook.* Say: *Look! She's a pilot.*
- Learners repeat after you.
- Show the pictures in random order and ask: *Is he a king? Is she a princess?* Learners answer.

2 We're going to a party! 36

- Point to the pictures. Tell learners to listen and point to Lucy.
- Play the audio a few times. Ask: *What is Lucy wearing?*
- Play the audio again. Point to the characters and pause after each line for learners to repeat.

Audioscript: Track 36

Lucy: Hi, I'm Lucy. I'm with my family. We're making clothes. We're going to a party. I'm a pretty princess and I'm wearing a gold dress. My brother is wearing a silver jacket. He's a superhero.

Brother: Look at me! I'm flying.

Lucy: Look at Mum! Mum is a pilot!

Mum: Yes, I am! I'm wearing a pilot's hat. And here's my plane!

Dad: Look everybody. I'm a clown.

Grandma: Look at me. I'm a cook.

Grandpa: And I'm a king. Look at my ring!

Answers

Lucy is wearing a gold dress.

3 Topic vocabulary 37

- Focus on page 53. Direct learners' attention to the words and pictures. Play the audio and mime to make the meanings clear.
- Play the audio. Pause after each word. Learners point to the correct picture and repeat.
- Write the words on the board. Read the words together with the learners. Check for correct pronunciation.
- Pause the audio at the beep. Learners look at the picture on page 52 again. They listen and decide who is who in the picture.
- Play the recording at least twice. Play again and stop after each sentence to give the class time to think and decide on their answers.

Audioscript: Track 37

Speaker: dress

    shirt

    trousers

    jacket

    skirt

    shoes

    glasses

    hat

Lucy: Hi, I'm Lucy. I'm wearing a gold dress. Can you find me?

Boy: Hi, I'm Lucy's brother. I'm wearing a silver jacket. Can you find me?

Mum: Hello. I'm Lucy's mother. I'm wearing black trousers and a pilot hat. Can you find me?

Dad: Hello, I'm Lucy's father. I'm wearing a colourful shirt and big shoes. Can you find me?

Grandma: Hello, I'm Lucy's grandma. I'm wearing a white skirt, a white top and a white hat. Can you find me?

Grandpa: Hello, I'm Lucy's grandpa. I'm wearing a silver ring. Can you find me?

Answers
Top, from left to right: Dad, Brother.
Bottom, from left to right: Grandma, Lucy, Mum, Grandpa.

 For further practice, see Activities 1 and 2 in the Activity Book.

4 Who are you?

- Read the question and the answers with the class. Learners decide who they are and what they are wearing.
- Model the activity. Invite learners to ask you questions.
- Then they circulate, asking and answering the questions.
- If available, learners could dress up with real clothes or accessories as a variation on this activity.

Answers
Learners' own answers.

 For further practice, see Activity 3 in the Activity Book.

Writing tip

- Direct learners to the **Writing tip** on page 53.
- Write *I am* on the board. Explain how we join the words together to say: *I'm*. Write *I'm* on the board. Ask learners to find other examples of *I'm* in the Learner's Book on page 53.

5 Draw and write

- Give learners pencils, crayons and paper and/or magazines, scissors and glue. Ask them to make a picture of themselves in party clothes.
- Learners should write a description of what they are wearing at the foot of the picture. You may wish to save their work in their portfolios.

Answers
Learners' own answers.

[AB] **For further practice, see Activity 4 in the Activity Book.**

Wrap up

- **Portfolio opportunity:** Ask learners to show their pictures to the class and describe what they are wearing. You may wish to save their work in their portfolios.
- Play a guessing game to review topic vocabulary. Begin to draw an item of clothing very slowly. Learners guess what it is.

Activity Book

1 Clothes

- Read the words as a class. Learners then write the words next to the correct picture.
- Help learners through the activity, especially with the spelling of new words.

Answers
1 jacket
2 shirt
3 shoes
4 trousers
5 skirt
6 hat
7 dress
8 glasses

2 Draw and write

- Learners draw their pictures. Once they have finished, ask them to show their pictures and say who they are before attempting the writing. Circulate, helping with spelling as necessary.

Answers
Learners' own answers.

3 Word snake

- Remind learners what a word snake is. Model one or two words and then ask learners to carry on individually or in pairs. Check as a class.

4 Who am I?

- Ask learners to read the sentences aloud. Then they match them to the correct picture.

Answers
1 c
2 a
3 b

I can say what I am wearing.

- Direct learners' attention to the self-evaluation question at the top of page 40. Ask them to think and answer. Emphasise the importance of giving an honest answer.

Differentiated instruction

Additional support and practice

- **Clothes game:** Write six items of clothing on the board and give each a number, e.g. jacket 1, top 2. Divide the class into two teams. Put two of each item of clothing on the board in a pile on the floor. Learners line up in their teams. Place the pile of clothes a short distance away. Throw a dice. According to the number on the dice, the first member of each team runs to the pile, puts on the item and runs back to their team. The first to arrive with the correct item scores a point for their team.

Extend and challenge

- In small groups, learners make a collage of a boy or girl dressed for a party, then write a description of the picture on their poster.

Lesson 2: Find out more

Colourful quilts

Learner's Book pages: 54–55
Activity Book pages: 42–43

Lesson objectives

Listening: Listen to and follow instructions.

Speaking: Compare and contrast, practise vocabulary, talk about ways to have fun.

Reading: Read instructions.

Writing: Complete a conversation.

Critical thinking: Create and combine patterns.

Language focus: Present continuous, positive statements: *He's cutting triangles. She's cutting squares.*

Questions: *What are the children making? They're making …*

Vocabulary: shapes: *triangle, rectangle, square, circle; quilt, make*

Materials: Shapes made of card: a triangle, rectangle, square and circle; different coloured card for making shapes, scissors, glue, sheets of A4 paper; map of the world; large sheet of paper, crayons or pencils; clothes or pictures of clothes, a box for the clothes/pictures; pictures of quilts from magazines.

Learner's Book

📖 Warm up

- Guessing game: put items of clothing or pictures of clothes in a box on your table.
- Begin to take out an item of clothing or a picture, very slowly and ask: *What is it?*
- Learners guess. When they have said the correct answer, ask: *Is it (red)? What colour is it? Is it(big)?*

📖 Introduce vocabulary

- Introduce the shapes. Show each shape and say the word. Learners repeat.
- Ask learners to look around and find objects with similar shapes to the cards: the class board for a rectangle, etc.

1 Before you read

- Open books at page 54. Focus on the photo, read the explanation and explain what a *blanket* is. Show magazine photos, if available, of other quilts, e.g. on beds.
- Point at the quilt in the book and ask learners to look for different shapes. Ask, e.g. *How many triangles are there?*

Answers
There are squares, triangles and rectangles in the picture.

2 Read and listen 38

- Point to each picture in turn. Say, *This is Mei-Mei. She's from China. Where's China?*
- Invite learners to find China on the map or globe.
- Repeat with Kevin. Help learners find the USA on the map and trace the route from their country to the USA.
- Play the audio. Point to the pictures in turn and ask learners what the missing words are.
- Help them to write the missing words in their book.

Audioscript: Track 38
Speaker: Mei-Mei is from China.

　She likes red, black and white.

　She's cutting squares and circles.

Speaker: Kevin is from the USA.

　He likes orange, purple and …

　He's cutting triangles and …

For further practice, see Activity 1 in the Activity Book.

3 Paper shapes

- Focus on the picture. Point to the girl. Ask: *What is she doing?* Learners read the answer as a class.
- Point to the boy and ask the question. Learners look and answer.
- They write their answer. Help with spelling as necessary.
- Ask: *Can you see more shapes? What are they? How many (squares) are there? What colour are they?*

Answers
I'm cutting blue rectangles (or squares).

4 Making things with paper shapes

- Focus on the pictures and ask: *What are the children making?* Invite learners to answer.
- Then ask them to read the speech bubbles to see if they were right.
- Ask the class: *Can we make a quilt and a picture? Yes!*

5 It's your turn!

- Divide the class into pairs. Give learners pencils and crayons, card, scissors, glue and a sheet of paper, and ask them to decide what they are going to make.
- As they work, they ask and answer questions about what they are making.
- Circulate, asking questions about what they are doing. Check for correct pronunciation.

Answers
The boy is making a paper quilt.
The girl is making a picture.

 For further practice, see Activities 2, 3 and 4 in the Activity Book.

➦ Wrap up

- Write *Our class collage* on a large piece of paper. Ask learners to cut out shapes of different colours and create a class picture. Encourage them to make a landscape or a school scene.
- **Home–school link:** Learners show their quilt or picture to the family and describe it. They could ask parents and siblings to make a family picture or quilt, then bring it to the class and describe it. You may wish to keep it in their portfolios.

Activity Book

1 Make a quilt

- Explain the activity. When learners have finished, ask them to describe their quilt to the class. Ask: *How*

many (triangles) are there? What colour are they? They complete the sentences.

Answers
Learners' own answers.

2 A clown made of shapes

- Ask learners to count the shapes in the clown. Ask: *How many (triangles) are there?* They answer as a class, and then write the numbers.
- **Critical thinking:** This activity is especially useful for developing learners' observation skills and creativity, as they have to find patterns and combine elements to form new ones.

Answers
1 There are 2 squares.
2 There are 5 triangles.
3 There are 8 rectangles.
4 There are 5 circles.

3 Colour the shapes

- Learners read the sentences in **Activity 3** and colour the clown accordingly.

Answers
Learners' own answers.

4 Over to you

- Individually, learners decide on the identity of their clown. Help them with their writing if necessary. Ask individual learners to show their clown and describe it.

Answers
Learners' own answers.

I can talk about shapes.

- Direct learners' attention to the self-evaluation question at the top of page 42. Ask them to think and answer. Emphasise the importance of giving an honest answer.

Answers
Learners' own answers.

Differentiated instruction

Additional support and practice

- Ask learners to make illustrated vocabulary cards for shapes words. In pairs, Learner A shows a picture to Learner B. Learner B spells the word. They swap roles.

Extend and challenge

- 🔲 Learners write cards with the names of the countries they have located on the map so far, then place them on a map or globe.

Lesson 3: Letters and sounds

Short e

Learner's Book pages: 56–57

Activity Book pages: 44–45

Lesson objectives

Listening: Listen to a poem and a story, identify the sound of short **e**.

Speaking: Say a rhyme, act out a story.

Reading: Recognise words with short **e**, identify words that rhyme, read a story.

Writing: Write a class poem.

Critical thinking: Remember and recite a poem.

Language focus: Blending short **e** words, *Let's ...*
The verb *have: Meg has an egg.*

Vocabulary: *pen, egg, hen, gentlemen, tent, bed, teddy, jet*

Materials: Real objects, toys or pictures to represent the vocabulary above; card, pencils and crayons, glue.

Learner's Book

Warm up

- Remind learners of the poem they learned in **Unit 3 Lesson 3**. Say the poem as a class, miming as you recite.

Introduce new vocabulary

- Pick up the egg (or picture of an egg) and ask: *What is it? An egg.*
- Show the pen and say: *Look, a pen. An egg and a pen.*
- Do the same with the other words. Ask learners to repeat the words after you.

1 Listen and look 39

- Learners open books at page 56. Point to the pictures and say: *Let's listen.*
- Play the audio and point to the letter **e** and the pictures in turn.
- Play the audio again. Pause after each sound or word for learners to repeat.

> **Audioscript:** Track 39
> **Speaker:** e
> egg
> pen

2 Rhyming words

- Direct learners' attention to the rhymes and the pictures. Point to the pictures and revise the vocabulary.

- Ask learners to read the sentences aloud and find the rhyming words.
- Focus on picture 3 (a red bed). Ask learners what they see.
- Ask learners to think of a rhyme for picture 3. They may invent a name for the owner of the bed, e.g. *Ed, Fred, Ted: Fred has a red bed,* or simpler versions: *This bed is red.*

> **Answers**
> Picture 1 Hen/pen
> Picture 2 Meg/egg
> Picture 3 Learners' own answers

3 Higgledy Piggledy 40

- Direct learners' attention to the rhyme and the picture of the hen. Ask: *What's this? What colour is it? How many eggs can you see?*
- Tell the class they are going to listen to a rhyme. Play the audio. Point to the picture to help learners understand.
- Play the rhyme again. Pause after each line for learners to repeat.

> **Audioscript:** Track 40
> **Speaker:** Higgledy Piggledy
>
> My black hen.
> She lays eggs
> For gentlemen.
> Sometimes nine and sometimes ten.
> Higgledy Piggledy
> My black hen.

[AB] **For further practice, see Activities 1 and 2 in the Activity Book.**

4 Phonics story 41

- Focus on the pictures and ask learners to predict what happens in the story.
- Tell learners to listen and count the words that they hear with the short **e**.
- Play the recording a few times. Ask: *How many words are there?*
- Then play the recording again and point to each picture in turn. Mime to make the meaning clear to learners.
- Play the recording again. Invite learners to repeat after each line.
- As they grow more confident, invite them to act out the story in groups.

Answers
There are ten words: *Let's, tent, red, next, bed, teddy, jet, ten, pens, best.*

 For further practice, see Activity 3 and the Challenge in the Activity Book.

 Wrap up

- Collect all the sentences written by learners in the **Challenge**. Alternatively, ask them to write a sentence using two words from this selection: *hen, egg, bed, tent, pen, jet*. Write them on the board and create a class poem.
- Pass out paper and pencils. Learners write their name at the top of the paper, then copy the poem. Collect, write the date on the back, and save in the learners' portfolio.
- **Home–school link:** Learners teach *Higgledy Piggledy* to the family.

Activity Book

1 Which sound?

- Read the instructions and ask learners to read the words listed in the activity.
- With a partner, they classify the words according to the short sound. Check the answers as a class.
- **Critical thinking:** Remind learners of the concept of classifying elements in a chart.

Answers

Words with short e sound	Words with short a sound	Words with short u sound
pen	man	duck
ten	cat	sun
hen	hand	bug
bed	pan	rug

2 Rhyme

- Read the instructions and the sentences to learners. Invite them to say the words aloud before deciding which words rhyme with those in the sentences.

- **Critical thinking:** Remind learners of the concept of rhyme. Look for more rhyming words in previous units.

Suggested answers
Two words that rhyme with *hen: pen, ten*
Two words that rhyme with *bug: hug, rug*
Two words that rhyme with *can: man, pan*

3 Read and draw

- Ask learners to read the sentences aloud. Then they draw the missing items in the pictures.

Answers
Learners' own answers.

Challenge

- Remind learners of the sentences they read in the Learner's Book.
- Ask them to choose two words and think of a sentence. Invite some learners to say their sentences aloud. When they have finished, they write their sentences in the Activity Book.
- As a follow-up activity, learners can read their sentences to the class.

Answers
Learners' own answers.

I can read and write words with the short e sound.

- Direct learners' attention to the self-evaluation question at the top of page 44. Ask them to think and answer. Emphasise the importance of giving an honest answer.

Answers
Learners' own answers.

Differentiated instruction

Additional support and practice

- Learners write words they remember that contain the short **e**. They can also draw the pictures to match.

Extend and challenge

- Learners create a tongue twister with rhyming words. Give an example and invite them to write their own tongue twister using rhyming words from **Unit 4** and previous units.

Lesson 4: Use of English

Painting a mural

Learner's Book pages: 58–59
Activity Book pages: 46–47

Lesson objectives

Listening: Listen to and follow instructions, listen to and complete sentences.

Speaking: Sing a traditional song, speak about what people are wearing.

Reading: Read and draw.

Writing: Write a song following a pattern.

Critical thinking: See a pattern in a song in order to make a new one.

Language focus: Present continuous, present simple

Vocabulary: *paint, think, gold, star, city, town, bridge, building, beautiful, boat, tree*

Materials: Pictures of the items of vocabulary; pictures of London and London Bridge; map of the world; crayons and coloured pencils, sheets of A4 paper, file cards.

Learner's Book

☞ Warm up

- Divide the class into two groups and invite them to recite the poem they learned in **Lesson 3**.
- Groups take turns to recite and mime one line each.

☞ Introduce new vocabulary

- Show the pictures of items in turn. Say: *What is it? It's a star. What colour is it? Look at the city. This is our city/town.*
- When learners have seen all the words once, show the pictures in random order and have them say the words. Then write the words on the board.

1 Look and listen 42

- Learners open books at page 58. Focus on the picture. Say: *Look at Liz. These are her friends. What are they doing?* Learners answer.
- Tell learners they are going to listen to Liz and they have to say the missing words.
- Play the recording a few times. Ask learners which words are missing and write them on the board.
- Ask them to point at the words on the board. Learners then copy the words in their books.

Audioscript: Track 42

Liz: We're painting a picture on the wall. We're painting our city.

Our teacher is helping us.

My name is Liz. I'm painting a red jet.

Emily is painting a gold bridge.

Tina is painting silver stars.

Marcos and Rob are painting tall buildings.

I think our city is beautiful.

Answers
1 Liz is painting a red **jet**.
2 Emily is painting a gold **bridge**.
3 Tina **is painting** silver stars.
4 Marcos and Rob are painting tall **buildings**.
5 Liz thinks the city is **beautiful**.

AB For further practice, see Activities 1 and 2 in the Activity Book.

2 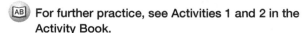 What are they wearing?

- Focus on the picture. In pairs, learners take turns to talk about the clothes the children are wearing.

Answers
Tina is wearing a purple shirt/T-shirt, a white skirt and brown socks/shoes.
Liz is wearing a green shirt/T-shirt, blue trousers and red socks/shoes.
Marcos and Rob are wearing red shirts/T-shirts, brown trousers and yellow hats/caps. Marcos is wearing brown socks/shoes and Rob is wearing green socks/shoes.
Emily is wearing an orange dress and brown socks/shoes.

3 🎵 A traditional song 43

- Focus on the picture. If learners are unfamiliar with London, explain that it is the most important city in England. Help them find London on a map. Show pictures of London and London Bridge.
- Tell learners that they are going to listen to a traditional English song. Play the recording twice to familiarise learners with the lyrics. Then play again and mime the actions to the song (see below).
- Play the song again. Learners sing and mime along.

Instructions for actions to accompany the song
London Bridge is falling down. Mime as if something big is crumbling and bend your knees and lower your body until your hands touch the floor. *Build it up* again by making the reverse movement. You may open and close your hands, fingers stretched as if miming something shiny to represent *silver* and *gold*.

Speaker: *London Bridge is falling down*

London Bridge is falling down,

Falling down, falling down.

London Bridge is falling down,

My fair lady.

Build it up with silver and gold,

Silver and gold, silver and gold.

Build it up with silver and gold,

My fair lady.

4 Make a new song

- In groups of three, ask learners to write a new verse for the song, replacing the colours and the building. Provide additional vocabulary on buildings if necessary.
- When they have finished, ask the groups of learners to sing their new song to the class.

> **Answers**
> Learners' own answers.

 For further practice, see Activity 3 in the Activity Book.

Wrap up

- Play a game of bingo to revise the vocabulary from **Lessons 3** and **4**.

Activity Book

1 Use *am, is* and *are*

- Remind learners of the use of auxiliaries by giving a few examples. For example, say: *I … making a quilt. Which word is missing? Is it I am, I is, I are?* Learners answer.
- Ask learners to read the text and complete it. Check as a class.

> **Answers**
> 1 We **are** painting a picture on the wall.
> 2 I **am** painting a red jet.
> 3 Tina **is** painting stars.
> 4 Marcos and Rob **are** painting tall buildings.

2 Read and draw

- Ask learners to read the sentences aloud. Then they draw the missing objects in the picture.

> **Answers**
> Learners' own answers.

3 Make up a song

- Tell learners to write a new song using the words provided in the activity. Circulate, helping as necessary.

- When they have finished, they sing the song to the class.
- **Critical thinking:** Before learners write their song, help them discover the similarity between the syllable patterns of *London Bridge* and the new song.

> **Answers**
> Learners' own answers.

I can say what people are doing.

- Direct learners' attention to the self-evaluation question at the top of page 46. Ask them to think and answer. Emphasise the importance of giving an honest answer.

> **Answers**
> Learners' own answers.

Differentiated instruction

Additional support and practice

- Ask learners to choose three words they like from this lesson. Give them three file cards, pencils and crayons. They make vocabulary cards.

Extend and challenge

- Learners make a small poster. They draw an imaginary city or town and label the buildings they know.

Lesson 5: Read and respond

Learner's Book pages: 60–63
Activity Book pages: 48–49

Lesson objectives

Listening: Listen to a traditional story.

Speaking: Make predictions about a story, discuss the plot, assess the characters, act out the story.

Reading: Read along as you listen, do a reading comprehension exercise, practise sight words, identify the title of a story, look for synonyms.

Writing: Choose words to complete sentences.

Language focus: Present continuous: *The elves are making the shoes; Let's help the shoemaker.* Phrases: *I'm very tired. New boots!* Questions with *who?* and *how?*: *Who are the characters? How do the elves help the shoemaker?*

Vocabulary: *elves, elf, shoemaker, shoes, boots, sleep, help, make, wake up, sell, watch, work, thank, lovely, morning, tired, happy*

Sight words: *is, are, look* and *these*

Materials: Pencils and crayons; glue, scissors, cotton, card for making puppets, optional: pieces of different coloured cloth for the clothes; a map of the world or globe; a large sheet of paper with a reproduction of the template of the letter in the Activity Book, a copy of **Photocopiable activity 7** for each learner.

Learner's Book

Warm up

- Sing *London Bridge is falling down*. Divide the class into two groups, with each group singing one verse.
- Choose one or two of the songs written by the learners and sing them all together.

Introduce vocabulary

- Use objects or pictures to introduce the new vocabulary: *elves, elf, shoemaker, shoes, boots.*
- Explain the different spelling of *elf* (singular) and *elves* (plural). Check for correct pronunciation.
- Show each picture in turn and ask: *What's this?* Learners answer.

1 Before you read 44

- Open books at page 60. Learners look at the pictures. Tell learners that this is a story from Germany. Help learners find Germany on a map or globe. Is it near or far away from their country? Are there any learners who come from that country?
- Tell learners what an *elf* is. Explain what a *magical creature* is. Ask what other magical creatures they know.
- **Critical thinking:** Ask: *Is this a song? Is it a poem? A story?* Why? Remind them of the difference between a song, a poem and a story. Ask if they have ever read a story about elves.
- Tell learners to look at the pictures and predict what the story will be about.
- Play the recording once. Learners listen and follow in their books to check if they were right.
- Read the two questions and ask learners to think about them as they listen again.
- Play the audio a few times. Discuss the answers as a class.
- Ask questions to check comprehension, e.g: *How many elves are there? What's the shoemaker doing? Is the shoemaker happy or sad?*
- Divide the class into groups A, B, C and D, and assign a character to each group, i.e. Group A the elves, Group B the shoemaker, Group C the narrator and Group D the customer. Invite more confident learners to act the story out for the class.

Answers
The elves help the shoemaker make some shoes to sell.
The shoemaker makes the elves new boots, jackets and hats.

Audioscript: Track 44
See Learner's Book pages 60–62.

2 Think about the story

- Read the first question. Explain what a title is and ask the class to find the title of this story.
- Go on reading one question at a time and elicit the answers from the learners.

Answers
The title of the story is *The elves and the shoemaker.*
The characters in this story are the elves, the shoemaker and the customers.
The elves help the shoemaker make some shoes to sell.
The shoemaker makes the elves new boots, jackets and hats.

[AB] **For further practice, see Activity 1 in the Activity Book.**

3 Clothes in the pictures

- Ask learners to read the clothes words aloud.
- Ask them to find the clothes in the pictures from **Activity 1**. Ask: *How many jackets can you see? What colour are they?*
- Learners point to the pictures in the book and answer.
- Learners read the story again and try to find the words. You may wish to explain that words that mean the same are called *synonyms.*

Suggested answers
All the following items are in the story:
Jacket: There are blue, yellow and red jackets. The shoemaker has a green jacket.
Trousers: There are red and yellow trousers.
Dress: There are red, yellow and blue dresses.
Shirt: There are white and blue shirts.
Hat: There are red, yellow, blue, brown, green and yellow, pink and yellow hats.
Shoes: There are red, brown, pink, blue, orange, purple and silver shoes.

Language detective

- Ask learners what things are *beautiful*. Then, tell them that they are going to play a game. They are language detectives.
- They have to read the story again and discover two words that mean the same as *beautiful*.
- The two words that mean the same as *beautiful* are *lovely* and *pretty*.

[AB] **For further practice, see Activities 2 and 3, and the Challenge in the Activity Book.**

4 Puppets

- Give each learner a copy of **Photocopiable activity 7**, pencils and crayons, pieces of cloth, cotton and card to make the puppets.
- When they have finished, divide the class into small groups. Learners act out the story with their puppets.
- **Home–school link:** Learners take their puppets home and retell the story to the family.

Words to remember

- Write the words *is, are, look* and *these* on the board.
- Learners look for the sight words in the text. How many times do they see the words? Make them count on their fingers.

🖙 Wrap up

- Ask the class what they would ask the elves for, e.g. clothes, toys, books? What would they give the elves in return?

Activity Book

1 The elves and the shoemaker

- Explain the activity. Ask learners to help you read the questions.
- Learners match the questions to the correct answers. Check answers as a class.
- **Critical thinking:** This is a good opportunity to ask learners to reflect on the structure of the story, characters, title, end, consequences of the characters' actions.
- **Values:** Discuss with learners the importance of helping people and being grateful. Did the elves expect any reward in return?

Answers
1 b
2 a
3 c
4 e
5 d

2 New clothes!

- Ask learners to label the picture with the clothes words. Tell them to refer to the **Word box** if they need to check the spelling.

Answers
Top to bottom: hat, jacket, trousers, boots.

3 Is it true?

- Learners read the sentences and circle *yes* or *no*. Check answers as a class.
- **Critical thinking:** Ask learners to read the story again before deciding. This will help them recall and process information more easily.

Answers
1 Yes
2 No
3 Yes
4 No

Challenge

Tell learners you are going to write a letter to the shoemaker.

- Put the poster with the template of the letter on the board.
- Elicit sentences to include from learners. Write them on the poster and correct the mistakes as a class. Learners try to include words from the **Challenge** in their letters.
- When it is finished, learners copy it into their Activity Books.
- **Critical thinking:** Explain how a letter is organised. Point to the different parts. Ask learners to find differences between a story and a letter.

Answers
Learners' own answers.

I can say what people are doing.

- Direct learners' attention to the self-evaluation question at the top of page 48. Ask them to think and answer. Emphasise the importance of giving an honest answer.

Answers
Learners' own answers.

Differentiated instruction

Additional support and practice

- Ask learners to choose two words they like from this lesson. Then ask them to make illustrated vocabulary cards for these words and post them on the word wall.

Extend and challenge

- Ask learners to write a thank you letter to a parent.

Lesson 6: Choose a project

What can we make with colours and shapes?

Learner's Book pages: 64–65
Activity Book pages: 50–51

Lesson objectives/assessment opportunities

Listening: Listen to comprehension items in the Activity Book quiz.

Speaking: Present your project to the class.

Reading: Read instructions, read sentences to do a matching exercise in the Activity Book quiz.

Writing: Write about a fashion model, a shape animal or a picture, write words in the Activity Book quiz.

Language focus: Unit 4 Review

Materials:

A Make a fashion model: Scissors, crayons or pencils, a copy of **Photocopiable activity 8** for each learner.

B Make a shape animal: Different coloured card, scissors, glue, pencils and crayons, sheet of A4 paper or card to glue the project on to.

C Draw a picture: Pencils and crayons, sheet of paper or card to draw on.

Learner's Book

Warm up

- **Guessing game:** Hold a dictation competition. Divide the class into two groups. Each group chooses and writes on pieces of paper five words they have learned in this unit. Group A dictates a word to one learner from Group B. This learner writes the word on the board. Give one point for each correct word.
- You may wish to have learners say the words instead of dictating them to make the activity more challenging.

Choose a project

- Learners choose an end-of-unit project to work on. Look at examples and help them choose. Move the children into groups, depending on their choices. Provide materials.
- **Informal assessment opportunity:** Circulate as learners work. Informally assess their receptive and productive language skills. Check for correct pronunciation and spelling of new vocabulary. Ask questions. You may want to take notes on learners' responses.
- If possible, leave the learner projects on display for a short while, then consider filing the projects, photos or scans of the work in learners' portfolios. Write the date on the work.

A Make a fashion model

- Read the directions in the Learner's Book and show the example model.
- Give learners the pencils and crayons and a copy of **Photocopiable activity 8**. They may also use old magazines and make a collage of clothes as their project.
- Help them write a description.

B Make a shape animal

- Read the directions. Give learners pieces of different coloured card, scissors, glue and sheets to glue their animal on.
- Learners cut out the shapes, make the animal and write a shape quiz for their friends following the model.

C Draw a picture

- Read the directions. Give learners pencils and crayons.

- When they have finished, learners write about their picture. Encourage learners to use the present continuous. Help with spelling as necessary.

Look what I can do!

- Review the *I can ...* statements. Learners demonstrate what they can do.

AB **For further practice, see the quiz in the Activity Book.**

Activity Book

Unit 4 Quiz: Look what I can do!

Listen **94** [CD2 Track 41]

- For items 1 to 6, learners listen to the audio and tick the correct picture. Do the first item as a class. Play the audio several times.

> **Audioscript:** Track 94
>
> **Narrator:** 1
>
> **Speaker:** I'm wearing trousers.
>
> **Narrator:** 2
>
> **Speaker 1:** What are you wearing?
>
> **Speaker 2:** I'm wearing a jacket.
>
> **Narrator:** 3
>
> **Speaker:** There is one rectangle.
>
> **Narrator:** 4
>
> **Speaker 1:** I can see three circles.
>
> **Speaker 2:** How many circles?
>
> **Speaker 1:** Three circles.
>
> **Narrator:** 5
>
> **Speaker:** Look at the boy. He's cutting.
>
> **Narrator:** 6
>
> **Speaker 1:** What is the girl doing?
>
> **Speaker 2:** She's painting.

Answers					
1 b	2 b	3 b	4 a	5 b	6 b

Read and write

- For items 7 and 8, learners match the words to the pictures. Demonstrate by tracing with your finger. For items 9 and 10, learners write the words to go with the pictures.

Answers			
7 b	8 a	9 *tent*	10 *bed*

5 On the farm

Unit overview

In this unit learners will:

- Say and ask what they can see on a farm
- Describe what they and others are doing on a farm
- Roleplay an interview
- Speak about life cycles
- Write a thank you letter.

Learners will build communication and literacy skills as they describe what they can see on a farm, what they and others are doing there, about life cycles of plants and animals, read and act out a story, sing a song and identify animal sounds, and read and act out a traditional story.

At the end of the unit, they will apply and personalise what they have learned by working in small groups to complete a project of their choice: making an alphabet chart, drawing a map of a farm, or learning a poem and teaching it to the class.

Language focus

Present continuous: positive and interrogative statements.

Present simple for describing natural cycles.

Vocabulary topics: farm animals, verbs associated to farm activities, verbs associated with growing, prepositions

Critical thinking

- Understanding the stages of a cycle
- Understanding life cycle diagrams
- Understanding spatial relationships
- Understanding a story map.

Self-assessment

- I can name things on a farm.
- I can say what people and animals are doing.
- I can say what I am doing.
- I can read and write words with the short **i** sound.

Teaching tip

Review the learners' work on the Activity Book quiz, noting areas where they demonstrate strength and areas where they need additional instruction and practice. Use this information to customise your teaching as you continue to **Unit 6**.

Lesson 1: Think about it

What can you find on a farm?

Learner's Book pages: 66–67

Activity Book pages: 52–53

Lesson objectives

Listening: Listen to a poem, listen for information.

Speaking: Ask and answer questions about what people are doing, practise theme vocabulary.

Reading: Recite and read a poem, read labels.

Writing: Write what you are doing.

Writing tip: Use of capital letters at the beginning of a sentence and full stop at the end.

Language focus: Present continuous statements and questions: *The boys are feeding the animals. Are you planting rice? What are you doing?*

Vocabulary: *farmer, tractor, stall, field, rice, wood, lettuce, strawberry, chick, hen, horse, cow, plant, pick, drive, carry, feed, help*

Materials: Real objects, toys or pictures to represent the vocabulary above; markers or coloured pencils, magazine photos of farm animals, scissors, glue, large sheet of paper.

Learner's Book

☞ Warm up

- Revise animal vocabulary from the previous units. Play a guessing game.
- Whisper an animal to a learner. They mime the animal and the class guesses what it is.

Think about it

- Show learners a picture of a farm. Ask them if they have ever been to one.
- Ask: *What can you find on a farm? Can you see birds / dogs? What things can you see?*
- Elicit answers from learners and provide English equivalents as necessary.
- Take advantage of this situation to teach: *How do you say … in English?*

☞ Introduce new vocabulary

- Show pictures to introduce *farmer, tractor, stall, field, rice* and *chick.*
- Hold up each picture, say the word and ask learners to mime and repeat after you.
- Show the pictures in random order and ask, e.g. *Is he a farmer?* Learners answer *Yes, he is / No, he isn't.*

1 Read and listen 45

- Open books at page 66. Focus on the picture. Ask: *What can you see in the picture? Can you see a tractor? A chick? What are they doing?*

- Point to the poem. Say: *Read and listen.* Play the audio a few times.
- Pause for learners to repeat each line and mime.
- Practise reciting the poem together.

Audioscript: Track 45

Speaker: *Farm poem*

Hello to the farmer,

Hello to the tractor,

Hello to the cows in their stall.

Hello to the fields,

Hello to the chicks,

Hello to you all!

---

2 ☺ Interviews with farm families 46

- Point to the TV reporter and ask: *Is she a farmer?* [*No, she isn't*].
- Say: *She's on the TV, she's a reporter. Look! She's asking questions. Let's listen.*
- Play the audio. Learners look at the pictures as they listen.
- Play the audio again. This time, learners find and point to the corresponding picture.
- Play again and pause after each line for learners to repeat and mime.
- Gradually, encourage learners to practise the conversations independently.

Audioscript: Track 46

Speaker: Good morning, sir. What are you doing?

Farmer: I'm driving a tractor. I'm carrying lots of wood!

Speaker: Hi there! What are you doing?

Boy 1: I'm feeding our cows. I like feeding them.

Speaker: Hello! What are you all doing?

Boy 2: We're feeding our hens. We feed them every day.

Speaker: Hi girls, what are you doing?

Girl 2: We're planting rice in our field. We're helping our family.

Speaker: Hi, what are you doing?

Young boy: I'm picking strawberries on our farm.

Speaker: Are you having fun?

Young boy: Yes! I love strawberries!

Answers
1 b
2 a
3 e
4 d
5 c

---

3 Topic vocabulary

- Focus on page 67. Direct learners' attention to the words. Play the audio and mime to make the meanings clear.
- Play the audio again. Pause after each word. Learners point at the correct picture and repeat.
- Write the words on the board. Read the words together. Check for correct pronunciation.
- Play the second part of the audio. Direct learners' attention to the pictures and the sentences.
- Learners say the missing word in each sentence.
- Learners look at the pictures on page 66 again. They listen again and point to the right picture.

> **Audioscript:** Track 47
> **Speaker:** feeding
>
>   planting
>
>   picking
>
>   driving
>
>   carrying
>
> The boys are feeding the …
>
> The man is driving a …
>
> The two girls are planting …
>
> The little boy is picking …

> **Answers**
> chicks
> tractor
> rice
> strawberries

[AB] For further practice, see Activity 1 in the Activity Book.

4 🗨 Act it out

- Learners take turns to choose a sentence from **Activity 3** and act it out.
- Their partner asks questions, e.g. *Are you planting rice?* [*Yes, I am / No, I'm not*]

[AB] For further practice, see Activities 2 and 3 in the Activity Book.

5 📝 [AB] Draw and write

- Discuss with learners how they can help on a farm. Elicit examples and provide extra vocabulary as necessary.

➡ Wrap up

- Learners recite the poem as a class.

Activity Book

1 Match the words

- Go to pages 52 and 53. Focus on the pictures. Ask learners to read the words and trace a line with their

fingers to the corresponding activity. They then draw the lines on the page.

> **Answers**
> **1** c
> **2** a
> **3** b

2 It's time to feed the animals!

- Explain the activity. Point to the **Word box** and ask learners to read and say the words. Then, read the first sentence. Learners say and write the others. Check answers as a class.

> **Answers**
> **1** She is feeding the cow.
> **2** He is feeding the hen.
> **3** They are feeding the horse.

3 Draw and write

- Ask learners to make a picture of themselves helping on a farm.
- When they have finished, they show it to the class and describe what they are doing. They then write a sentence to describe this underneath the picture.

> **Answers**
> Learners' own answers.

Writing tip

Remind learners of the use of capital letters and full stops in their writing.

I can say what people and animals are doing.
I can say what I am doing.

- Direct learners' attention to the self-evaluation question at the top of page 52. Ask them to think and answer. Emphasise the importance of giving an honest answer.

> **Answers**
> Learners' own answers.

Differentiated instruction

Additional support and practice

- In small groups, learners make a poster collage of a farm scene using a variety of materials and write a description of the images on their poster.

Extend and challenge

- 🗨 Young radio presenters. Learners choose roles following the example of **Activity 2** in the Learner's Book and roleplay interviews. They can also practise some conversation starters: *Hello, Good morning, Hi there! How are you? What are you doing? Are you having fun?*

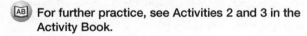

Lesson 2: Find out more

Life cycles

Learner's Book pages: 68–69
Activity Book pages: 54–55

Lesson objectives

Listening: Listen to and understand key information.

Speaking: Practise science vocabulary, talk about different life cycles.

Reading: Read about life cycles.

Writing: Complete a conversation.

Critical thinking: Understanding the stages of a cycle, understanding life cycle diagrams.

Language focus: Present simple, positive statements: *A tiny chick grows*

Vocabulary: *life cycle, chick, egg, seed, ground, bean, plant* (v. and n.), *grow, come out, eat, become, lay, start, inside*

Materials: Shopping basket or bag; items or pictures of the following foods: *butter, bread, milk, eggs;* pictures of key vocabulary: *life cycle, chick, seed, ground, bean, plant;* file cards, sheets of A3 paper, pencils and crayons, glue.

Learner's Book

Warm up

- Ask learners: *What comes from a farm?* Have a shopping bag of food items (see above) and discuss which food grows on a farm and which foods come from farm animals.

Introduce vocabulary

- Introduce key vocabulary: *life cycle, chick, egg, seed, ground, bean, plant.* Show the pictures and say the words. Learners repeat.
- Play a spelling game with the new vocabulary.

1 Before you read

- Open books at page 68. Focus on the picture and explain what it is.
- Ask learners to follow the arrows and explain what happens in each stage of the life cycle. Help with the necessary language and encourage learners to use key vocabulary.

> **Answers**
> There is an egg. The chick comes out of the egg. The chick eats and grows into a hen. The hen lays an egg.

Language detective

Mime as you read the sentence. Ask learners to find the hidden word.

2 Read and listen 48

- Focus on the pictures. Play the audio. Point to the pictures in turn.
- Play the audio again, miming the actions to help learners understand.
- Play the audio again, pause after each sentence and ask learners to repeat and mime.
- **Critical thinking:** Discuss with learners why the life cycle diagram looks as it does, and what the function of the arrows is. What do they show?

> **Audioscript:** Track 48
> **Speaker:** *The life cycle of a hen*
>
> A tiny chick grows inside an egg.
>
> The chick comes out of the egg.
>
> The yellow chick eats and grows.
>
> The chick becomes a hen. The hen lays an egg.

AB For further practice, see Activity 1 in the Activity Book.

3 Animals that lay eggs

- Focus on the pictures. Ask: *Does a (duck) lay eggs?*
- Learners answer: *Yes* or *No.*
- Encourage learners to offer more examples. Supply vocabulary as necessary.

> **Answers**
> The turtle, duck and fish lay eggs.

AB For further practice, see the Challenge in the Activity Book.

4 Before you read

- **Critical thinking:** Focus on the diagram. Invite learners to come up with an explanation. Tell them to compare with the life cycle of a hen for ideas.
- Help with the necessary language; encourage learners to use key vocabulary. Discuss as a class.

5 Read and listen 49

- Focus on the pictures. Play the audio. Point to the pictures in turn.
- Play the audio again, miming the actions to help learners understand.
- Play the audio again, pause after each sentence and ask learners to repeat and mime.

6 Things that grow from seeds

- Focus on the pictures. Ask: *Does an (ant) grow from seeds?*
- Learners answer: *Yes* or *No.*
- Encourage learners to offer more examples. Supply vocabulary as necessary.

Answers
Sweetcorn (**a**), trees (**b**) and flowers (**d**) grow from seeds.

7   Draw and write

- Ask learners to look at the pictures. Elicit the order of the life cycle from the pictures.
- Learners draw and write their answers in Activity 2 of the Activity Book.

Answers
See Activity 2 in the Activity Book.

[AB] **For further practice, see Activity 2 in the Activity Book.**

Wrap up

- Play *Hangman* to review topic vocabulary.

Activity Book

1 Spell the words

- Focus on the pictures and the scrambled letters. Ask learners to write the words with the letters in the correct order.
- Check as a class by asking one learner to spell a word while another writes on the board.

Answers
1 eggs
2 hen
3 chick
4 seeds
5 bean
6 plant

Challenge

- Direct learners' attention to the challenge question. Encourage them to offer examples, e.g. *duck and goose.* Accept other options if correct: *a swan, a fish, a frog,* etc.

Answers
duck, goose, swan, fish, frog etc.

2 Life cycle

- Ask learners to complete the life cycle diagram in their Activity Book.

Suggested answers
Life cycle of a goose / duck
A baby gosling / duckling grows inside the egg.
The gosling / duckling comes out of the egg.
The gosling / duckling eats and grows.
The gosling / duckling becomes a goose / duck.
The goose / duck lays an egg.

I can name things on a farm.

- Direct learners' attention to the self-evaluation question at the top of page 54. Ask them to think and answer. Emphasise the importance of giving an honest answer.

Answers
Learners' own answers.

Differentiated instruction

Additional support and practice

- Ask learners to make word cards for key vocabulary. In pairs, they draw a mini poster of a life cycle and label it with their word cards.

Extend and challenge

- [image] Learners look for information about the life cycle of a tree. They make a mini poster and label the parts.

Lesson 3: Letters and sounds

Short i
Learner's Book pages: 70–71
Activity Book pages: 56–57

Lesson objectives

Listening: Listen to a tongue twister and a story, identify the sound of short **i.**

Speaking: Say a tongue twister, act out a story.

Reading: Recognise words with short **i**, identify words that rhyme, read a story.

Critical thinking: Memorise and act out a story, understanding what a tongue twister is, creating a tongue twister from a model.

Language focus: Blending short **i** words
Vocabulary: *big, pick, sister, sick, sheep, stick, fig, kick, fish, fix, swing, tail, fin, wing*

Materials: Real objects, toys, pictures or word cards to represent the vocabulary above; card, pencils and crayons, glue, copies of **Photocopiable activity 9**.

Learner's Book

 Warm up

- Remind learners of the poems they have learned so far in the Learner's Book. Ask them to choose one and recite it.

1 Listen and look 50

- Learners open books at page 70. Point to the pictures and say: *Let's listen.*
- Play the first part of the audio and point to the letter **i** and the two pictures in turn.
- Play this part of the audio again. Pause after each sound or word. Learners repeat.
- Focus on the incomplete word and ask learners to add the short **i** sound. Ask: *What's the name of the animal?*
- Ask learners to listen to the sound **ch** and think of two more words with the same sound. Focus on the pictures.

> **Answers**
> Chick.
> Two more words beginning with the sound **ch** are *children* and *chair*.

> **Audioscript:** Track 50
> **Speaker: 1** i
>
> big
>
> pick
>
> **Speaker:** ch
>
> chick

2 Tongue twisters 50

- Direct learners' attention to the tongue twisters. Ask them if they know any in their mother tongue. Say a few together.
- **Critical thinking:** Ask learners to look at the tongue twisters and think about their structures. What makes them different from a sentence?
- Focus on the tongue twisters and the pictures. Point to the pictures and present the vocabulary.
- Ask learners to listen carefully to the second part of Audio 50. Play each tongue twister a few times in turn.
- Learners repeat each tongue twister.

- When learners are more confident, you may organise class competitions in small groups to see who can say the tongue twisters the fastest without making any mistakes.

> **Audioscript:** Track 50
> **Speaker: 2** Six sisters sing to six sick sheep.
>
> Six sisters sing to six sick sheep.
> Six sisters sing to six sick sheep.
>
> How many sticks can a big chick kick?
> How many sticks can a big chick kick?
> How many sticks can a big chick kick?
>
> Pick a big fig.
> Pick a big fig.
> Pick a big fig.

 For further practice, see Activity 1 in the Activity Book.

3 Phonics story 51

- Direct learners' attention to the story and the pictures. Say: *Look! This is a fish. What's the fish doing? Let's listen.*
- Play the audio. Point to each picture to help learners understand.
- Play the story again. Pause after each line for learners to repeat.
- Tell learners to listen and put up their hands when they hear words with the short **i** sound.
- Invite learners to point to the pictures and read the story along with the recording.

> **Audioscript:** Track 51
> **Speaker:** *Fix-it Fish*
>
> This fish can fix things.
>
> He is fixing a ship.
>
> **Fix-it Fish:** I can fix this ship.
>
> **Speaker:** He is fixing a swing.
>
> **Fish:** Can you fix it?
>
> **Fix-it Fish:** Yes, I can.
>
> **Speaker:** He can fix tails, fins, and wings.
>
> **Seagull:** Can you fix my wing, please?
>
> **Fix-it Fish:** Yes, I can. Just a minute.
>
> **Fish + seagull:** Thank you, Fix-it Fish!
>
> **Fix-it Fish:** You're welcome!

For further practice, see Activity 2 in the Activity Book.

4 Puppets

*   Give learners **Photocopiable activity 9**.
*   When they have finished making their puppets, they act out the story.

 For further practice, see Activity 3 in the Activity Book.

➡ Wrap up

*   Ask the class to look at previous units and find words with the short **i** sound. Copy them on the board. Tell them to choose a few, e.g. five, and challenge them to say the words very quickly.
*   **Home–school link:** Learners teach their tongue twisters to their families. They could also ask parents what tongue twisters they used to say when they were children.

Activity Book

1 Read and draw

*   Ask learners read the sentences in the Activity Book and complete the picture according to the instructions.
*   When they have finished, ask them to show their picture to the class and say what there is in it.

Answers
Learners' own answers.

2 Rhyming words

*   Ask learners to read the words. Then they draw lines between the words that rhyme.

Answers
chick / stick
duck / truck
swing / ring

Challenge

*   Ask learners to give two example words. Remind them to look back at previous lessons in the book to see if they can find any words.

Suggested answers
wing and *sing*

3 Animal crossword puzzle

*   Remind learners of how to solve a crossword puzzle. They work in pairs and write the answers in their Activity Book.
*   Check the answers as a class.

Answers
1 down	cat
1 across	chick
2 fish	
3 duck	
4 bug	
5 hen	

I can read and write words with the short i sound.

*   Direct learners' attention to the self-evaluation question at the top of page 56. Ask them to think and answer. Emphasise the importance of giving an honest answer.

Answers
Learners' own answers.

Differentiated instruction

Additional support and practice

*   Learners write words they remember that contain the short **i**. They can also draw pictures to represent the words.
*   They could also create a new tongue twister using words from previous units, to include in their portfolios.

Extend and challenge

*   Learners create a crossword puzzle following the example in the Activity Book. Invite them to use words from **Unit 5** and previous units.

Lesson 4: Use of English

Farm activities

Learner's Book pages: 72–73
Activity Book pages: 58–59

Lesson objectives

Listening: Listen and identify animals, listen and complete sentences.

Speaking: Sing a song, speak about the growth of plants, ask and answer questions about farm activities.

Reading: Read and complete sentences.

Writing: Write a song following a pattern, complete sentences, answer questions, label pictures.

Writing tip: Short forms: *he's, she's, it's, they're.*

Language focus: Present continuous, present simple
Prepositions: *above, under*
Vocabulary: Vegetables: *carrots, onions, potatoes, tomatoes, peppers, beans; ground, jar, roots, stem, leaf, leaves; horse*

Materials: Real vegetables, objects, toys or pictures to represent the vocabulary above; a shopping bag, a copy of **Photocopiable activity 10** for each learner; crayons and coloured pencils, file cards; dry beans, a glass jar or sealable plastic sandwich bag for each learner, cotton or paper towels for each jar / bag, onions, plastic flower pots or containers, toothpicks, stickers or labels.

Learner's Book

Warm up

- Divide the class into three groups and have a tongue twister competition. Each group says a tongue twister from **Lesson 3** as fast as possible, trying to make the fewest mistakes.

Introduce new vocabulary

- Put the pictures of vegetables or the real vegetables in a shopping bag. Show them in turn. Say: *Look, a (carrot). What colour is it? Do you like (carrots)?*
- Show the pictures or point at the vegetables in random order and ask learners to say the words.
- Then write the words on the board under the heading *Vegetables.*
- **Personalisation:** Ask learners if they like eating vegetables. What vegetables do they like? Do they eat vegetables every day? Do they think they are good for them?

1 Growing vegetables

- Learners open books at page 72. Focus on the picture. Ask: *What do you see in this picture? What is the girl / boy / dog doing?*
- Read the sentences. Use the picture to explain *above / under.* Discuss the answers as a class.
- Write learners' answers in a two-column chart under the headings *Above the ground* and *Under the ground.*
- Learners copy the chart in their notebooks.

> **Answers**
> Vegetables that grow above the ground: tomatoes, peppers, seeds.
> Vegetables that grow under the ground: carrots, onions, potatoes.

2 Ask and answer

- Focus on the picture. In pairs, learners ask and answer questions about the picture following the examples on the page. Model yourself first with a few learners.

> **Answers**
> Learners' own answers.

[AB] For further practice, see Activities 1 and 2 in the Activity Book.

3 [AB] Grow a bean plant

- Explain that you are going to grow a bean plant in a jar that will look like the picture in their books.
- Introduce the vocabulary of the different parts of the plant: *leaf, leaves, bean, stem, seed, roots.*

> **Suggested answers**
> Inside the bean there are seeds. When we planted the seed it grew roots and a stem. A leaf grew from the stem and after that several leaves grew on the bean plant. Later there were also beans on the plants.

[AB] For further practice, see Activity 3 in the Activity Book.

4 Noisy animals 52

- Focus on the picture and ask learners to identify the animals. Teach the word *horse* if necessary.
- Tell learners you are going to listen to the animals and identify them.
- Play the audio. Learners point to the correct animal and say what animal it is.
- Tell learners you are going to sing a song about old MacDonald, the farmer in the picture.
- Play the song a few times. Ask learners to make the animal noises for the cow, the duck and the sheep.

> **Audioscript:** Track 52
> **Speaker:** moo
> **Speaker:** woof woof
> **Speaker:** baa
> **Speaker:** cluck cluck
> **Speaker:** neigh
> **Speaker:** quack quack

Speaker: *Old MacDonald had a farm*

Old MacDonald had a farm, E-I-E-I-O.
And on that farm he had a cow, E-I-E-I-O.
With a *moo moo* here and a *moo moo* there,
Here a *moo,* there a *moo,* everywhere a *moo moo!*
Old MacDonald had a farm, E-I-E-I-O.

Old MacDonald had a farm, E-I-E-I-O.
And on that farm he had a duck, E-I-E-I-O.
With a *quack quack* here and a *quack quack* there,
Here a *quack,* there a *quack,* everywhere a *quack quack!*
Old MacDonald had a farm, E-I-E-I-O.

Old MacDonald had a farm, E-I-E-I-O.
And on that farm he had a sheep, E-I-E-I-O.
With a *baa baa* here and a *baa baa* there,
Here a *baa,* there a *baa,* everywhere a *baa baa!*
Old MacDonald had a farm, E-I-E-I-O.

Old MacDonald had a farm, E-I-E-I-O.
And on that farm he had a cow, E-I-E-I-O.
With a *moo moo* here and a *moo moo* there,
Here a *moo,* there a *moo,* everywhere a *moo moo!*
Old MacDonald had a farm, E-I-E-I-O.

Answers
cow, dog, sheep, hens, horse, ducks, then all the animals together.

5 📝 🎵 Sing some new verses

• Ask learners to write a new verse for the song choosing another farm animal.
• Sing the new verses as a class.

Answers
Learners' own answers.

👉 Wrap up

• Play a guessing game to revise the vocabulary from **Lessons 3** and **4**. Learners draw an item of vocabulary very slowly on the board. The class then asks questions until they guess what it is.
• You may turn this into a class competition, with the learners divided into two groups. The first group to guess the correct item of vocabulary gets a point.
• **Home–school link:** Learners take their plants home, explain to their family what they have done and tell them the names for the parts of the plant in English.

Activity Book

1 What are they doing?

• Focus on the picture and ask learners to describe what they see.
• They then read the first question aloud, trace the line to the answer and read it.
• Check the answers as a class when learners have finished.

Answers
1 d
2 b
3 c
4 e
5 a

Writing tip

Explain that we can join together some words. Remind them of *I'm / I am.*

2 Missing words

• Explain the activity and go through the example answer with learners.
• Read the second question and ask learners to say what words are missing.
• They complete the task independently. Check answers as a class.

Answers
1 No, they're **not.**
2 Yes, it is.
3 No, it's **sleeping**.
4 Yes, they are.
5 No, she's **feeding the horse**.

3 Growing a plant

• Soak dried beans overnight to help speed up sprouting. Give each child a jar or a sealable plastic sandwich bag.
• Help learners place damp cotton balls or damp paper towel in it.
• They then place two or three beans between the damp towel or cotton ball and the side of the jar or sandwich bag so the bean is easily seen.
• Learners write their name on a sticker and label their jar or bag.
• They check their bean seeds often and draw and / or write their observations in a journal. Beans should sprout within 3 to 4 days.
• At the end of this process they draw the plant in their Activity Book and label the parts of the plant.
• **Critical thinking:** This activity is a good opportunity to develop learners' observation skills and help them draw conclusions from these observations.

Answers
Learners' own answers.

I can say what people and animals are doing.

• Direct learners' attention to the self-evaluation question at the top of page 58. Ask them to think and answer. Emphasise the importance of giving an honest answer.

Answers
Learners' own answers.

Differentiated instruction

Additional support and practice

Photocopiable activity 10

1 With learners, plant one or two onions in soil with the top of the bulb above the soil. The onion stems will grow rapidly in the first week.

2 'Plant' another one or two onions in water. This will let learners watch the onion roots grow. Poke toothpicks into the side of the onion and balance it at the top of a jar. Fill the jar with water so that it just touches the tiny roots at the base of the onion.

3 Count the leaves growing from each onion bulb. Invite learners to sniff the onion leaves. How do they smell?

4 Measure the plants using standard and non-standard measuring tools. Learners cut a strip of paper to the length of the longest onion leaf.

Extend and challenge

- Learners use their onion leaf measurement strips to make a cumulative graph that shows how their onion leaves are growing over a number of days. If learners are doing standardised measuring, use a ruler to measure the length of the leaves.

Lesson 5: Read and respond

Learner's Book pages: 74–77

Activity Book pages: 60–61

Lesson objectives

Listening: Listen to a traditional story.

Speaking: Make predictions about a story, discuss the plot, assess the characters, act out the story.

Reading: Read along as you listen, do a reading comprehension exercise, practise sight words, identify the title of a story.

Writing: Choose words to complete sentences.

Critical thinking: Understand a story map, understand outcomes, identify and compare characters, compare stories and find common features.

Writing tip: short forms *I'm, We're.*

Language focus: Present continuous: *I am making the bread, now.* Polite forms: *Can you please help me…? Will you…?* Phrases: *Sorry, I'm busy. It's delicious! You're very helpful.*

Sight words: *am, me, you* and *too*

Vocabulary: *make bread, pick wheat, grind, helpful, eat, wash the dishes, sweep the floor*

Materials: Real objects, toys, pictures or word cards to represent the vocabulary above; a map of the world or globe; another version of the story; pencils and crayons, sheets of A4 paper.

Learner's Book

☞ Warm up

- Sing *Old MacDonald had a farm.* Divide the class into three groups, with each group singing one stanza.
- Choose three of the stanzas written by the learners and sing them all together.

☞ Introduce vocabulary

- Use the objects or pictures to introduce the new vocabulary: *make bread, pick wheat, grind, helpful, eat, wash the dishes, sweep the floor.*
- Show each of your pictures in turn and ask: *What's (Pat) doing?* [Answer: *He's / She's making bread.*]

1 Before you read 53

- Open books at page 74. Learners look at the pictures. Tell learners that this is a story from Russia. Help learners find Russia on a map or globe. Is it near or far away from their country? Are there any learners who come from that country?
- **Critical thinking:** Ask: *Is this a song? Is it a poem? A story? Why?* Remind them of the differences between a song, a poem and a story.
- **Personalisation:** Say: *This is a folktale.* Explain what a folktale is. Ask learners if they know any folktales in their own language. What's the title? Who are the characters? Invite learners to talk about the folktale.
- Read the title. Tell learners look at the pictures to predict what the story will be about.
- Play the recording once. Learners listen and follow in their books to check if they were right.
- Point at the pictures and ask questions to check comprehension, e.g: *What's the hen doing? Is the chick helping her?*
- **Critical thinking:** Ask learners who the main character is, and who the other characters in the story are.

Audioscript: Track 53

See Learner's Book pages 74–76.

2 Think about the story

- Read one question at a time and elicit the answers from the learners.
- **Values:** Being helpful
- Focus on the second question: *Which characters aren't helpful?* Ask learners: *Are you helpful at home? What do you do at home?*
- Discuss the end of the story. Ask learners about stories they know with happy and sad endings.

- **Critical thinking:** Ask learners what would have happened if the characters had behaved differently, or if one of the characters had been helpful at the beginning of the story.

Answers
Little Red Hen, Duck and Chick are the characters in the story. Duck and Chick are not helping Little Red Hen at the beginning of the story, but at the end they are helping her.
It's a happy ending because everyone enjoys the bread. This is because Duck and Chick agree to help Little Red Hen when they have eaten the bread.

 For further practice, see Activities 1, 2 and 3 in the Activity Book.

3 Story map Little Red Hen

- Explain that a story map shows the order that things happen in a story. Read the sentence and ask learners to look at the pictures. Ask them if the pictures are in order or not.
- **Critical thinking:** Ask learners to look at the story map again and re-tell the story from it.

Answers
1 Little Red Hen is picking wheat.
2 Little Red Hen is grinding wheat.
3 Little Red Hen is making bread.
4 Everyone is eating the bread.
5 Chick and Duck are washing the dishes and sweeping the floor.

4 ⊗ Same and different

- Ask learners if they know another version of the story. Ask them to tell it.
- In case they don't, you can look at: http://www. enchantedlearning.com/stories/fairytale/littleredhen/ story/
- **Critical thinking:** On the board and with the help of learners, create a Venn diagram comparing the two versions of the folktale. Ask learners to pinpoint similarities and differences.

Answers
Learners' own answers.

Writing tip

- Remind learners of how to write short forms. Revise the short forms they have learned in this unit.
- Tell learners to look for *I'm* / *We're* in the story. They can make word cards with the full and short forms they have learned in **Unit 5**.

5 ⊗ Act it out!

- Divide the class into small groups and assign a character to each group member. They act out the story in their groups.
- You may invite more confident groups to act out the story for the class.

Words to remember

- Write the words *am, me, you* and *too* on the board.
- Learners look for the sight words in the text. How many times do they see the word? Tell them to count on their fingers.
- You may ask learners to make word cards for these words.

Answers
am appears 4 times (7 including contraction in *I'm*)
me appears 6 times
you appears 7 times
too appears 3 times

⇨ Wrap up

- Ask the class if they know another story with a 'moral', i.e. a lesson to be learned. Encourage them to tell the story.
- **Home–school link:** Learners tell the story to their family. They may look for information about Russia together.

Activity Book

1 Little Red Hen

- Explain the activity. Learners look at the pictures and write in the missing words.
- Check answers as a class.

Answers
1 Hen
2 is
3 bread
4 are
5 Chick, Duck

2 Is it true?

- Explain the activity. Model the first question. Read it and ask: *Yes or no?* Elicit the answer from learners.
- Learners continue working independently. Check as a class.

Answers
1 yes
2 no
3 no
4 yes
5 no

3 Favourite character

- Ask learners to read the story again, choose their favourite character and write who it is in their Activity Book.
- Ask a few learners about their choice of character.
- Invite them to ask a friend. Then they record their answer in the Activity Book. Do they both have the same favourite character?

Answers
Learners' own answers.

I can say what people and animals are doing.

- Direct learners' attention to the self-evaluation question at the top of page 60. Ask them to think and answer. Emphasise the importance of giving an honest answer.

Answers
Learners' own answers.

Differentiated instruction

Additional support and practice

- Ask learners to choose another story from the book and make a story map for it.

Extend and challenge

- Ask learners to look for information about Russia: the name of the capital city, Russian animals and plants, typical Russian clothes or food. They make pictures and word cards, and label a map. Then they display the map in the classroom.

Lesson 6: Choose a project

What can you find on a farm?

Learner's Book pages: 78–79
Activity Book pages: 62–63

Lesson objectives

Listening: Listen to comprehension items in the Activity Book quiz.

Speaking: Present your project to the class, describe a farm, say what the animals are doing.

Reading: Read instructions, read and learn a poem, read sentences to do a matching exercise in the Activity Book quiz.

Writing: Write words to complete an alphabet chart, write words on a map of a farm, write words in the Activity Book quiz.

Language focus: Unit 5 Review

Materials:

A Make an alphabet chart: Scissors, crayons or pencils, file cards, old magazines, glue, poster paper.

B Draw a map of a farm: Different coloured card, scissors, glue, pencils and crayons, sheet of A3 paper or card to glue the project on.

C Learn a poem: Optional picture to illustrate *weed*.

Learner's Book

Warm up

- Play a vocabulary revision game: divide the class into two groups. One learner from each group in turn mimes an action or an animal, the other group guesses the correct word. Give a point for each correct guess.

Choose a project

- Learners choose an end-of-unit project to work on. Look at the learner-made samples and help them choose. Move the children into groups depending on their choices. Provide materials.

A Make an alphabet chart

- Read the instructions in the Learner's Book and show the example model.
- Give learners the pencils and crayons and cards to make their own chart. They may also use old magazines and cut out pictures to do this.
- Learners look for words beginning with different letters of the alphabet and make cards for the poster.
- Help them write the letter and the word for each picture.
- They glue their cards on the poster paper in alphabetical order.

B Draw a map of a farm

- Read the directions. Give learners pieces of different coloured card, scissors, glue and pencils and crayons to make the animals and plants.
- They glue everything onto their poster and decorate it.
- Learners then show their map to friends. They describe what there is and what the animals are doing.

C Learn a poem

- Use a picture or mime to teach the word *weed*.
- Read the poem with the learners, then help them recite it independently without reading it off the page.
- They practise their poem, miming as they recite it.
- Learners then teach the poem to others in the class.
- **Informal assessment opportunity:** Circulate as learners work. Informally assess their receptive and productive language skills. Check for correct pronunciation and spelling of new vocabulary. Ask questions. You may want to take notes on their responses.
- If possible, leave the learner projects on display for a short while, then consider filing the projects, photos or scans of the work, in learners' portfolios. Write the date on the work.

Look what I can do!

- Review the *I can …* statements. Learners demonstrate what they can do.

Answers
big

[AB] **For further practice, see the quiz in the Activity Book.**

Unit 5 Quiz: Look what I can do!

Listen 95 [CD2 Track 42]

- For items 1 to 6, learners listen to the audio and tick the correct picture. Do the first item as a class. Play the audio several times.

Audioscript: Track 95

Narrator: 1

Speaker: The girls are feeding the chicks.

Narrator: 2

Boy: I'm picking an apple.

Narrator: 3

Speaker: I can see an apple tree, a hen, and three cows.

Narrator: 4

Speaker 1: What are you doing?

Girl: I'm planting a bean seed.

Narrator: 5

Speaker 1: Is the duck sleeping?

Speaker 2: No it's not. The duck is swimming.

Narrator: 6

Speaker 1: Are the horses eating carrots?

Speaker 2: No, they're not. They're eating apples.

Answers
1 b   2 c   3 c   4 a   5 b   6 b

Read and write

- For items 7 and 8, learners match the words to the pictures. Demonstrate by tracing with your finger. For items 9 and 10, learners write the words to go with the pictures.

Answers
7 a   8 b   9 *six*   10 *fish*

6 My five senses

Unit overview

In this unit learners will:
- Say and ask how they can use their senses
- Describe what they and others can do
- Speak about favourite things
- Speak about how things feel
- Compare things
- Do a class survey.

Learners will build communication and literacy skills as they describe how they can use their senses, read and act out a story, recite a poem, compare things, and read and act out a traditional story.

At the end of the unit, they will apply and personalise what they have learned by working in small groups to complete a project of their choice: doing a class survey, making a book, or writing a poem about a special place.

Language focus

Can with sense verbs to express ability: *I can play the piano.*

Review of present simple questions

Comparison of adjectives: *cold-er*

Vocabulary topics: Sense verbs, musical instruments, adjectives that describe how things feel, body parts, ordinal numbers

Critical thinking
- Comparing and finding similarities and differences
- Understanding sequential order
- Making inferences
- Understanding how to make a class survey.

Self-assessment
- I can talk about my five senses.
- I say how things sound and feel.
- I can compare things.
- I can read and write words with the short **o** sound.

Teaching tip

Review the learners' work on the Activity Book quiz, noting areas where children demonstrate strength and areas where they need additional instruction and practice. Use this information to customise your teaching as you continue to **Unit 7**.

Lesson 1: Think about it

How do we use our five senses?

Learner's Book pages: 80–81

Activity Book pages: 64–65

Lesson objectives

Listening: Listen to a song, listen for information.

Speaking: Ask and answer questions about what people can do, practise theme vocabulary.

Reading: Read and recite a poem.

Writing: Write about how learners can use their senses.

Language focus: *Can* with sense verbs to express ability: *I can play the piano.*

Vocabulary: Revision: *eyes, ears, nose, mouth; see, hear, smell, like, senses, touch, taste;* musical instruments: *piano, violin, bass drum, saxophone, triangle*

Materials: Real objects, instruments or pictures to represent the vocabulary above; pictures of landscapes, a bottle of perfume, markers or coloured pencils, A3 sheets of paper.

Learner's Book

Warm up

- Revise vocabulary from previous units by putting vocabulary cards or objects around the classroom. Play *I Spy …*

Think about it

- Show learners a picture of a landscape. Ask: *What things can you see in the picture?*
- Show learners a bottle of perfume, open it, point at your nose and say, e.g. *It smells nice.*
- Play some music, cup your hands around your ears and ask, e.g. *Can you hear the music?*
- Tell learners that we have five senses; mime to make your meaning clear.

Introduce new vocabulary

- Show pictures to revise *eyes, ears, nose, mouth.*
- Hold up each picture, say the word and ask learners to mime and repeat after you.
- Draw the outline of a face on the board and ask individual learners to draw the eyes, the ears, the nose and the mouth on the face.

1 Read and listen 54 [CD2 Track 1]

- Open books at page 80. Play the audio a few times. Learners point to the different parts of their faces.
- Play the audio again. Pause after each line for learners to repeat.
- Practise reciting the poem together.
- Ask: *What can you do with your ears / eyes / nose?*

Audioscript: Track 54

Speaker: *Two little eyes*

Two little eyes to see all around.

Two little ears to hear each sound.

One little nose to smell what's sweet.

One little mouth that likes to eat.

2 In the park 55 [CD2 Track 2]

- Point to the picture and ask learners what they can see.
- Say: *Let's listen and point.* Play the audio once.
- Mime to help learners understand. Learners look at the pictures as they listen.
- Play the audio again. This time, learners find and point to the corresponding picture. Explain and write the new words on the board, e.g. *cherries, toy rabbit, band.* Read the words together. Check for correct pronunciation.

Audioscript: Track 55

Speaker: It's a beautiful day in the park. The sun is shining. I can hear birds singing.

Look! I can see the birds up in the trees. A little boy and his dad are smelling the flowers. Mmm. The flowers smell nice! A family is eating red cherries. The cherries taste sweet! The baby is touching a toy rabbit. It feels nice and soft.

On the stage, a band is playing. Can you hear the music?

Listen now! A train is coming. Can you hear it?

Wow! That train is loud.

Answers

Learners point to *park, sun, birds, trees, boy, dad, flowers, family, red cherries, baby, toy rabbit, band, train.*

3 Topic vocabulary 56 [CD2 Track 3]

- Focus on page 81. Direct learners' attention to the words: *see, hear, smell, taste, touch.* Play the audio and mime to make the meanings clear.
- Play the audio again. Pause after each word so that learners can point at the correct picture and repeat.
- Write the words on the board. Read the words together. Check for correct pronunciation.
- Play the second part of the audio. Direct learners' attention to the pictures.
- Play the audio again. Learners say the missing word in each sentence.
- Focus on the poem on page 80 again. Ask learners to identify which sense is not in it.

> **Answers**
> *Eyes, ears, nose, mouth, hands.*
> *Touch* is not in the poem.

4 Your five senses

- Learners look at the picture and discuss the statement, then report back to the class.

> **Answers**
> *See:* baby, family, trees
> *Hear:* birds, train, band
> *Smell:* flowers
> *Touch:* toy rabbit
> *Taste:* cherries

[AB] **For further practice, see Activities 1 and 2 and the Challenge in the Activity Book.**

5 [AB] [♪] Sing a song 57 [CD2 Track 4]

- Tell learners you are going to listen to some musicians playing their instruments.
- Play the audio and mime the instruments in time to the music. Learners mime along and repeat the words.
- Play the second part of the audio several times encouraging learners to sing and mime along.

[AB] **For further practice, see Activity 3 in the Activity Book.**

6 Guessing game

- Play the guessing game in pairs or as a class competition. Learners can win a point for every instrument they guess correctly in the game. At the end the winning learner is the one with the most points.

⮕ Wrap up

- Ask the class what they can touch, hear, smell, taste and see in the school.

Activity Book

1 My five senses

- Ask learners to read and complete the sentences with the words in the box.
- When they have finished, you may ask individual learners to read their sentences out to the class.

> **Answers**
> 1 see
> 2 hear
> 3 smell
> 4 taste
> 5 touch

Challenge

- Learners look around them and write about what they can see. Then ask them to pay attention to sounds they can hear and write about them. Circulate, helping with additional vocabulary if necessary.

> **Answers**
> Learners' own answers.

2 Read and colour

- Explain the activity. Learners look at the picture carefully and colour it according to the instructions.
- Ask: *What else do you think the people in the picture can smell / taste / hear, etc?*

> **Answers**
> Learners should colour the roses yellow, the cherries red and the guitar blue.

3 Musical instruments

- Ask learners to look at the pictures, read the words and trace with their fingers to the corresponding instrument. They then draw the lines.
- Check answers as a class.

> **Answers**
> 1 b
> 2 f
> 3 c
> 4 a
> 5 e
> 6 d

I can talk about my five senses.

Direct learners' attention to the self-evaluation question at the top of page 64. Ask them to think and answer. Emphasise the importance of giving an honest answer.

> **Answers**
> Learners' own answers.

Differentiated instruction

Additional support and practice

- Ask learners if they play any musical instruments. If any of them do, invite them to bring it to the next lesson and play the instrument to the class.
- Are there any traditional musical instruments in the learners' countries? What are they? Invite learners to find out and make a mini poster in groups showing these traditional instruments.

Extend and challenge

- Individually or in pairs, learners think of a place (their garden, home, school, the beach, etc.) and write what they can see, hear, smell, touch, taste in that place. Then they draw a mini poster and write the sentences.

Lesson 2: Find out more

Using your five senses

Learner's Book pages: 82–83
Activity Book pages: 66–67

Lesson objectives

Listening: Listen to and understand key information.

Speaking: Say how things sound and feel, speak about differences.

Reading: Read and understand a dialogue.

Writing: Make a list, complete sentences, write a dialogue.

Critical thinking: Explore different sensations, classify.

Language focus: Review of present simple questions: *Do you like…? How does it feel?*

Vocabulary: *soap, mango, smoke, ball, sock, bat, paper clip, soup, ring, worm, noodle;* adjectives: *soft, hard, round, flat, short, long, big, little*

Materials: Real objects or pictures to represent the vocabulary above; fluffy toys, a stone, a plastic toy, small plastic or rubber balls; one small bag and a small box per pair of learners; assortment of small objects.

Learner's Book

➭ Warm up

- Tell learners to return to the picture in **Lesson 1**. Ask: *What can you see in the park?* In pairs, they say as many things as possible.
- As a class, they sing the song in **Lesson 1** again.

➭ Introduce vocabulary

- Introduce key vocabulary: *soap, mango, smoke, ball, sock, bat, paper clip.* Show the objects or pictures and say the words. Learners repeat.

1 ➭ Seeing

- Point at the pictures in turn and ask: *What are the children doing? What can you see in the picture?*
- Ask learners to look at the pictures and find five differences. Then they complete the sentences. Check as a class.

> **Answers**
>
> | Picture A | Picture B |
> |---|---|
> | 1 There are 2 girls and 1 boy. | 1 There is 1 girl and 2 boys. |
> | 2 The boy is playing the drums. | 2 The boy is playing a guitar. |
> | 3 The table is a circle. | 3 The table is a rectangle. |
> | 4 There are 2 drums. | 4 There are 3 drums. |
> | 5 The girls are playing guitars. | 5 The boy and the girl are playing the drums. |

2 Smelling

- Point to the pictures and revise the vocabulary. Ask: *What's this? Is it an apple or a mango?*
- Focus on the speech bubbles and read the dialogue with learners.
- In pairs, they ask and answer questions about the pictures using the dialogue as a model.
- As a class, learners make a list of favourite smells.
- In their notebook, learners write a sentence for each smell and illustrate it.

> **Answers**
> Learners' own answers.

AB For further practice, see Activity 1 and the Challenge in the Activity Book.

3 AB Touching

- Ask learners to touch different objects, e.g. fluffy toys, a stone, a plastic toy, a rubber ball, to introduce the key vocabulary: *soft, hard, round, flat, short, long, big* and *little*.
- Learners then give more examples of things that are soft, hard, etc.
- Ask learners to close their eyes. Say: *Imagine you're in bed and it's dark. You touch something (soft). What is it?* Elicit answers from learners.
- Focus on the picture of the girl in bed on page 83. Ask learners to read and choose their answer.
- Focus on the pictures and ask: *How do these objects feel?* Learners answer.
- **Critical thinking:** Learners identify different materials and become aware of the sensations produced by each. They explain what they feel and give reasons for opinions. They also discuss the similarities and differences between materials.

> **Suggested answers**
> *Ball:* hard, round
> *Pencil:* hard, short
> *Bat:* hard, flat, long, big
> *Paper clip:* hard, flat, little
> *Socks:* soft, short

4 Touch and tell

- Explain the activity. Model the dialogue and mime with one learner.
- Give each pair of learners a small paper or cloth bag and an assortment of objects to play the game.

AB For further practice, see Activity 2 and the Challenge in the Activity Book.

5 Hearing: Shake and listen

- Give pairs a small box and an assortment of small objects.
- Learners play the game in the same way they did with the bag, except they shake and listen to guess. Model with one learner first.

Wrap up

- Ask individual learners to think of an object and describe it to the class, e.g. *It feels hard and cold. It's grey.* The class has to guess what it is, e.g. *a stone.*
- **Home–school link:** Learners ask family members about their favourite smells and keep a record in their notebooks. Then, they report back to the class. You may wish to keep the work in their portfolios. They can also play the 'Touch and tell' game with their families.

Activity Book

1 Smelling

- Focus on the pictures and the question. Ask a few example questions: *Do you like the smell of (flowers)?* Learners answer and then write in their Activity Book.

> **Answers**
> Learners' own answers.

Challenge

- Focus on the challenge question. Encourage learners to offer examples and write them in their Activity Book. Help with the vocabulary if necessary.

> **Answers**
> Learners' own answers.

2 Touching

- Point to the objects and elicit the words from learners. Model one example with a learner.
- Learners then work independently to complete the exercise. Check answers as a class.

> **Suggested answers**
> A ring: *hard, round, little*
> A worm: *soft, round, long*
> A door: *hard, flat, big*
> An apple: *hard, round, little*
> A quilt: *soft, flat, big*
> A noodle: *soft, round, long*

Challenge

- Focus on the challenge question. Encourage learners to offer examples and write them in their Activity Book. Help with additional vocabulary if necessary.

> **Answers**
> Learners' own answers.

I can talk about my five senses.
I can say how things sound and feel.

- Direct learners' attention to the self-evaluation questions at the top of page 66. Ask them to think and answer. Emphasise the importance of giving an honest answer.

Differentiated instruction

Additional support and practice

• Ask learners to make word cards for key vocabulary. They choose two or three words and make illustrated word cards.

Extend and challenge

• Learners make a table with headings of the following categories: *soft, hard, round, flat, short, long, big* and *little*. They circulate around the classroom or, if possible, in the school garden, looking for things to include in each category.

Lesson 3: Letters and sounds

Short *o*

Learner's Book pages: 84–85

Activity Book pages: 68–69

Lesson objectives

Listening: Listen to a rhyme and a story, identify the sound of short **o**.

Speaking: Say a rhyme, act out a story.

Reading: Recognise words with short **o**, identify words in a word snake, read a story and answer questions about it.

Critical thinking: Memorise and recall a story, listen to and act out a rhyme.

Language focus: Blending short **o** words, preposition: *on*

Vocabulary: *log, frog, fox, rock, hot, oil, pot, popcorn, grin, sizzle, hop, pond, nod, tap*

Materials: Real objects, toys, pictures or word cards to represent the vocabulary above; card, pencils and crayons, glue, copy of *Tic-tac-toe* board from **Photocopiable activity 11** for each learner.

Learner's Book

🔄 Warm up

• Write on the board a few words with different short sounds the class has learnt so far. Ask learners to find words which have the same short sounds in them.

1 Listen and look 58 [CD2 Track 5]

• Learners open books at page 84. Point to the pictures and say: *Let's listen.*

• Play the audio and point to the letter **o** and the pictures in turn.

• Explain the preposition *on*. Give a few examples of sentences with *on* using objects in the classroom: *The (pencil) is on the (book).*

• Play the audio again. Pause after each sound or word. Learners repeat.

• Ask learners to make sentences using the words in the audio.

Audioscript: Track 58

Speaker: o

  on

  box

  frog

Suggested answer

The frog is on the box.

---

2 Which picture?

• Focus on the pictures and introduce the new words (*log, fox, rock, hot*).

• Ask learners to read the sentences aloud. Then they match them to the pictures.

Answers

1 c

2 b

3 a

 For further practice, see Activity 1 in the Activity Book.

3 Popcorn 59 [CD2 Track 6]

• Tell learners you are going to listen to a rhyme. Point to the different words in the picture, e.g. *pot, popcorn,* to make sure learners know the meaning.

• Play the audio a few times. Mime to make the meaning clear.

• Play the audio again. Pause after each line for learners to repeat.

• Ask learners to find and say the words that have the short **o**, then write the words in their notebooks.

• **Personalisation:** Ask learners if they have ever eaten popcorn? Do they like it? Where do they buy it? Do they make it at home with their families?

• **Critical thinking:** Invite learners to memorise the rhyme and act it out as a class or individually. Insist on them using mime, as this will help them remember the lines of the rhyme.

Audioscript: Track 59

Speaker: You put the oil in the pot,

  And you let it get hot.

  You put the popcorn in,

  And you start to grin.

  Sizzle, sizzle, sizzle, sizzle,

  Pop, pop, pop!

Answers

There are four words with the short **o** sound: *pot, hot, popcorn* and *pop.*

---

4 [AB] Phonics story 60 [CD2 Track 7]

- Direct learners' attention to the pictures. Ask: *What can you see in the pictures? Are the sticks hard or soft? Look at the fish! They're in the pond. Do you think the water is cold? Let's listen.*
- Play the audio. Point to each picture to help learners understand.
- Play the audio again. Pause after each line for learners to repeat and mime.
- Tell learners to listen again and put up their hands when they hear words with the short o sound.
- Then they say the words.
- Invite learners to point to the pictures and read the story along with the recording.

> **Audioscript:** Track 60
> **Speaker:** *Tick, tock, hop!*
>
> Bob, the frog, hops to the pond.
>
> Hop, hop, stop. Hop, hop, stop.
>
> **Bob the frog:** Hi. My name is Bob.
>
> **Speaker:** Bob hears an odd sound.
>
> Tick, tock. Tick, tock.
>
> He sees his friend Fred, the fox.
>
> **Bob the frog:** Hi, Fred. What's that?
>
> **Fred the fox:** It's a clock.
>
> **Speaker:** Fred hits a rock with two sticks.
>
> Tap-tap, bop! Tap-tap, bop!
>
> **Bob the frog:** I like that sound!
>
> **Speaker:** The fish in the pond hear the sound.
>
> Flip, flop. Flip, flop.
>
> **Fish:** We like that sound!
>
> **Speaker:** Two rabbits hear the sound.
>
> Hop, hop, hop! Hop, hop, hop!
>
> **Rabbit:** Come on, Bob! You can hop, too.
>
> **Speaker:** Tick, tock. Hop, hop, hop!
>
> We can dance to the sound of the clock!

> **Answers**
> There are 12 words: *Hop/s, Bob, frog, pond, stop, tock, fox, clock, rock, bop, flop, on.*

[AB] **For further practice, see Activities 2 and 3 in the Activity Book.**

5 Act it out

- Divide the class into groups and ask learners to choose a role.
- They act out the story.

Wrap up

- Ask the class to say the rhyme.
- Pass out paper and pencils. Learners write their name at the top of the paper, then create a tongue twister using words from this lesson. Collect their work, write the date on the back, and save in learners' portfolios.
- **Home–school link:** Learners recite and teach the story to their family. They can also act out the story with parents and siblings.

Activity Book

1 Word snake

- Remind learners what a word snake is and ask them to find the words in it. Then they write them next to the correct picture.

> **Answers**
> **1** box **2** fox **3** sock **4** clock
> **5** log **6** frog **7** rock **8** top
>
>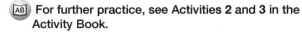
> asboxpthfrogksslsockprgtoparrfoxbbzclockjsrockqulog

2 Tick, tock, hop!

Ask learners to read the story again.

- Read the first question aloud and ask learners to choose the right answer. Check answers as a class.

> **Answers**
> **1** a clock
> **2** Fred the fox
> **3** the fish in the pond
> **4** the rabbits and the frog

3 Read and colour

- Read the instructions with learners. They draw and colour the picture according to the instructions.
- When they have finished, ask a few learners to show and describe their picture.

> **Answers**
> Learners' own answers.

I can read and write words with the short o sound.

- Direct learners' attention to the self-evaluation question at the top of page 68. Ask them to think and answer. Emphasise the importance of giving an honest answer.

> **Answers**
> Learners' own answers.

Differentiated instruction

Additional support and practice

• Learners write words they remember that contain the short **o**. They can also draw pictures to represent the words.

Extend and challenge

• Play *Tic-tac-toe* as a class.

• **Directions:** Give learners a list of at least nine vocabulary words and copy of the *Tic-tac-toe* board from **Photocopiable activity 11**. Each learner chooses nine words to write and illustrate on their *Tic-tac-toe* board. The game is played by a pair of learners sharing one board. If each learner has a board, the pair of learners will be playing with two boards per pair. Each player has a different set of game markers, e.g. five buttons or five paper clips, five black or red checkers. Players take turns choosing a space in which to place a marker. Before placing the marker on the space, the player must read the word in that space aloud. If they read the word correctly, they 'win' the square. The first player with three markers in a row wins.

Lesson 4: Use of English

Comparing things

Learner's Book pages: 86–87
Activity Book pages: 70–71

Lesson objectives

Speaking: Compare how things are, taste and feel.

Reading: Read and complete sentences, follow instructions.

Writing: Complete sentences, answer questions.

Writing tip: Comparative forms: adding **-er** to form comparatives, spelling rules.

Critical thinking: Observe and compare things, draw conclusions.

Language focus: Comparative forms of adjectives

Vocabulary: adjectives: *tall, small, fast, sweet, juicy, cold; elephant, horse, mouse, car, jam, cake, yogurt, ice cream, watermelon, apple*

Materials: Real objects, pictures or cards to represent the vocabulary above; one small box, a rubber band and a ruler for each learner, an assortment of objects that can be used as drums.

Learner's Book

Warm up

• In groups, learners act out the story in **Lesson 3**.

Introduce new vocabulary

• Show the objects or pictures in turn and say: *Look, an elephant. What colour is it? Is it big or small?*

• Show the pictures in random order and have learners say the words, then write the words on the board.

1 Taller and faster

• Learners open books at page 86. Look at the pictures in turn and read the sentences. Mime to make the meanings clear.

• Ask the learners the questions. Discuss the answers as a class. Introduce new vocabulary, if necessary.

• Write the learners' suggestions on the board and make full sentences, e.g. *A giraffe is taller than a tree.*

• Learners copy the sentences in their notebooks and draw a picture for each one.

• **Critical thinking:** Ask learners to look for objects in the classroom or the school yard and compare their sizes and lengths. You may wish to use pictures to increase the options. They may also compare buildings in their town. This exercise will help develop awareness of different dimensions.

> **Suggested answers**
> A building is taller than a tree.
> A jet is faster than a car.

2 Tasting and feeling

• Focus on the first pair of pictures. Ask: *Do you like (jam)? Is (jam) sweet? What other things are sweet? Is (ice cream) cold? Do you like (ice cream)? What about (yogurt)?*

• Ask the question and model the answer with a learner.

• Learners ask and answer in pairs. Then they write the answers in their notebooks.

> **Suggested answers**
> I think jam is sweeter.
> I think ice cream is colder.
> I think watermelon is juicier.

Writing tip

• Focus on the rules. Write a few adjectives on the board, e.g. *fast, tall, pretty.* Ask learners how to spell the comparative forms. They write them on the board.

3 The sounds of a guitar 61 [CD2 Track 8]

• Tell learners that you are going to listen to a guitar. If you have a guitar, you could bring it to the class and show the different sounds it can make. Play the first part of the recording. Explain the kinds of sounds a guitar can make. Ask learners if they have understood. Play again if necessary.

• Proceed to the second part of the audio. Play a few times if necessary.

Audioscript: Track 61

Speaker: A guitar can make loud sounds and quiet sounds. It can make high sounds and low sounds.

Listen carefully. Is the second sound louder or quieter?

Narrator: 1

Narrator: 2

Narrator: 3

Narrator: Is the second sound higher or lower?

Narrator: 1

Narrator: 2

Narrator: 3

Answers
Louder or quieter?
1 The second sound is louder.
2 The second sound is quieter.
3 The second sound is louder.
Higher or lower?
1 The second sound is higher.
2 The second sound is lower.
3 The second sound is lower.

4 Make a guitar

- Explain that you are going to make a guitar. Give the materials to the learners and explain how to make it. Refer to the picture.
- **Instructions for making a guitar:** Place a ruler so that it stands upright or diagonal in a small box with no lid, then loop a rubber band around the box and the ruler. (The ruler serves as the neck of the guitar. The rubber band is stretched into a triangle shape.)
- The learner uses their left hand to pinch the rubber band a couple inches from the rim of the box and stretch it taut. With their right hand, they pluck the stretched length of rubber band.
- Read each question in turn, ask learners to 'play' their guitar and listen to the sounds it makes.

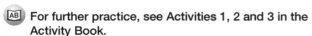 For further practice, see Activities 1, 2 and 3 in the Activity Book.

5 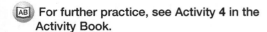 Make two drums

- Ask learners what things can make the sound of a drum, e.g. the chairs, a table, the board, a box.
- Focus on the picture and identify more objects that learners can use. They choose two and play their 'drums'.
- Learners then discuss why one is drum is louder than the other.

For further practice, see Activity 4 in the Activity Book.

Wrap up

- Play a spelling game to revise the vocabulary of **Lessons 3** and **4**.
- **Home–school link:** Learners draw their family and write sentences to compare who is taller/shorter: *Dad is taller than Mum. My sister is shorter than me.* etc.

Activity Book

1 Louder, sweeter, softer

- Read the first question with the learners and elicit the answers. Ask learners to complete the task independently. Check answers as a class.

Answers
Learners' own answers.

2 Write and draw

- Ask individual learners to read the sentences and decide on their answers. They then draw pictures that correspond to their answers.
- When they have finished they show and describe their work to the class or a partner.

Answers
Learners' own answers.

3 Adding -er

- Focus on the rules and remind learners of the examples they wrote for Learner's Book **Activity 2**.
- Ask individual learners to read each sentence in turn. Elicit the answers from the class.
- Learners complete the sentences in their Activity Book.

Answers
2 This hat is pretty but this hat is **prettier**.
3 Her hair is long, but her sister's hair is **longer**.
4 This horse looks funny, but this horse looks **funnier**.

4 Read and draw

- Explain the activity to the learners. Discuss ways to make the flower prettier and the monster scarier. Learners draw and colour their pictures.

I can compare things.

- Direct learners' attention to the self-evaluation question at the top of page 70. Ask them to think and answer. Emphasise the importance of giving an honest answer.

Answers
Learners' own answers.

Differentiated instruction

Additional support and practice

- Learners make illustrated word cards for the comparative forms of the adjectives they have learnt in this unit: *softer, harder, colder*, etc.

Extend and challenge

- Learners look for information and pictures of animals and compare them, e.g. *whale/shark, giraffe/elephant, worm/snake*. They make mini posters and write their sentences.

Answers

a teeth
b Jeep
c tree
d wheel
e bees
f a sleeping sheep
g knees
h seeds

2 How many?

- Read the questions. Ask learners to look at the picture carefully and count what they can see.
- They write the answers in their Activity Book.
- Ask individual learners to read their answers to the class.

Answers

1 There are 3 wheels. (2 visible Jeep wheels, one against the house)
2 There are 3 sheep.
3 There are 5 bees.

3 Rhyme

- Ask learners to read the words, then circle the words that rhyme.

Answers

1 a, b
2 b, c

Challenge

- Ask learners to find words that rhyme.
- **Critical thinking:** Extend work with rhyme by asking learners to work in pairs and find sets of rhyming words with other sounds. Invite them to use the book as a resource and explore previous units.

Suggested answers
seed: feed
feel: wheel
Jeep: sheep

4 Word snake

- Remind learners what a word snake is and ask learners to find the words in it. Then they write them next to the correct picture. Give help to learners that cannot find the missing word in the word snake.

Answers
ghkneeckkeeprsfeedbaagseobee
heppabeepwheeletdeersleepo

The word that is not in the word snake is *tree*.

I can read and write words with the long *e* spelling *ee*.

- Direct learners' attention to the self-evaluation question at the top of page 80. Ask them to think and answer. Emphasise the importance of giving an honest answer.

Answers
Learners' own answers.

Differentiated instruction

Additional support and practice

- Learners create a crossword puzzle using words from **Unit 7**.

Extend and challenge

- Learners create a story of their own following the model of in this lesson.

Lesson 4: Use of English

Describing things

Learner's Book pages: 100–101
Activity Book pages: 82–83

Lesson objectives

Listening: Listen to a poem and a song, listen to and complete sentences.

Speaking: Sing a song, describe things, count objects, give instructions, discuss information.

Reading: Read a poem and a song.

Writing: Write a poem, complete sentences, answer questions.

Critical thinking: Combine shapes and colours to construct an image, make a poem from a model.

Writing tip: Write the size word before the colour word.

Language focus: Imperatives, adjective word order: *number + size + colour + noun*, revision of numbers, shapes and size words

Vocabulary: *a ride, deep, sea, sails, middle, down, go round, wipers, money, chatter, bell*

Materials: Pencils and crayons, old magazines, glue, scissors, one A3 sheet of paper for each learner, copies of **Photocopiable activity 14** for each learner.

Learner's Book

 Warm up

- Play *Hangman* with the class to revise shape and colour words.

1 My big blue boat 68 [CD2 Track 15]

- Learners open books at page 100. Focus on the picture. Ask: *What can you see in this picture? What colour is the boat?*
- Play the audio and ask learners to follow the poem in their books.
- Play the audio again and mime to the poem; learners mime along with you.
- Play the audio once more, pausing after each verse for learners to repeat.
- **Instructions for mime actions** to accompany the song *My big blue boat*: Signal '*come*' with your hand and move one arm slowly up and down to mime sailing. Spread your arms to show something big around you, and look down and point to show '*deep*'. Point at yourself to mime '*my*', and make a triangle in the air with two fingers to show the sails.

> **Audioscript:** Track 68
>
> **Speaker:** Come for a ride in my big blue boat,
> My big blue boat, my big blue boat.
> Come for a ride in my big blue boat,
> Out on the deep blue sea.
>
> My big blue boat has two red sails,
> Two red sails, two red sails.
> My big blue boat has two red sails,
> Two red sails.

2 Draw a sailing boat

- Tell the class you are going to draw some pictures of coloured shapes. Give the class instructions: *Draw a big blue circle. Draw two small green triangles.* etc.
- Ask a few learners to come to the board and give similar instructions to the class. The other learners write the descriptions.
- Point out the order of the words which you use to describe the shapes: *number + size + colour + noun*
- Focus on the instructions and the pictures. Read them and draw the boat on the board to make the meaning clear.
- Give learners a sheet of paper. In pairs, they take turns to give instructions. Their partner draws the boat.
- **Critical thinking:** Invite learners to be creative and combine shapes and colours to create new designs.

3 Describe it

- Focus on the pictures and ask learners to choose one and describe it to their partner.
- Their partner decides which picture it is.

> **Answers**
> Learners' own answers.

 For further practice, see Activities 1, 2, 3 and 4 in the Activity Book.

4 The wheels on the bus 69 [CD2 Track 16]

- Focus on the picture and revise and introduce new words to the learners: *wheels, go round, wipers, money, chatter, bell.*
- Tell learners you are going to sing a song.
- Play the song a few times. Learners mime and sing along.

> **Audioscript:** Track 69
>
> **Speaker:** *The wheels on the bus*
>
> The wheels on the bus go round and round,
> round and round, round and round.
> The wheels on the bus go round and round,
> All day long.
>
> The wipers on the bus go swish, swish, swish …
>
> The money on the bus goes chink, chink, chink …
>
> The mums on the bus go chatter, chatter, chatter …
>
> The dads on the bus go ssh, ssh, ssh …
>
> The bell on the bus goes ding, ding, ding …

5 Make a car park mural

- Give each learner an A3 sheet of paper, pencils and crayons.
- They draw their car park. They may also use cut-outs from magazines and glue the cars they cut out in the car park.
- When they have finished, they write a few sentences to describe the poster.
- They then show it to the class and describe it.

☞ Wrap up

- Sing *The wheels on the bus* in groups. Divide the class into groups and assign a stanza to each to sing together.
- **Home–school link:** Learners teach their family the song and they sing it together. They can also show them their poem and recite it for them.

Activity Book

1 Colour a sea picture

- Focus on the picture and explain the activity. Ask learners to describe what they see.
- They then colour their picture and then complete the sentences with the correct colour word.

> **Answers**
> Learners' own answers.

2 Write about your picture

- As preparation for this activity, ask learners to show and describe their picture from **Activity 1** to the class.
- Then, they fill in the missing words to complete the description in their Activity Book.

> **Answers**
> Learners' own answers.

Writing tip

- Remind learners about the correct order of words in a description. Ask them to look at the poem and give similar examples.

3 My big blue boat

- Focus on the poem and read it as a class.
- Ask learners to circle size words and underline colour words. Check as a class.
- Practise reciting the poem in pairs.

> **Answers**
> Learners circle the word *big*, and underline the words *blue* and *red*.

4 Write your own poem

- Ask learners to write a new poem using the model in the Activity Book and the words in the box.
- When they have finished, they read the poem. They could also draw a picture to illustrate it.
- **Critical thinking:** Ask learners to look at the structure of the poem and use it as a model for their own ideas.

> **Answers**
> Learners' own answers.

I can say what colour and size something is.

- Direct learners' attention to the self-evaluation question at the top of page 82. Ask them to think and answer. Emphasise the importance of giving an honest answer.

> **Answers**
> Learners' own answers.

Differentiated instruction

Additional support and practice

- **Hidden words:** In pairs, ask learners to choose two words they have learned so far in this unit. They write the letters for each in scrambled order on slips of paper, e.g. *lehew*. They then exchange their words with another pair and write the words correctly, e.g. *wheel*. You may turn this activity into a class competition.

Extend and challenge

- Do **Photocopiable activity 14** as a class.

Lesson 5: Read and respond

Learner's Book pages: 102–105
Activity Book pages: 84–85

Lesson objectives

Listening: Listen to different ways to travel.

Speaking: Speak about different ways to travel.

Reading: Read along as you listen, do a reading comprehension exercise.

Writing: Make a chart, do a **true** or **false** exercise.

Critical thinking: Compare and find differences and similarities, make a chart, classify things according to a rule, understand the concept of building words from prefixes.

Writing tip: Short forms *I'm, We're.*

Language focus: Prefixes, *there is / there are,* prepositions: *up, down,* revision of present simple and *can*

Sight words: *go, can, up, down*

Vocabulary: Vehicles: *hydrofoil, underground train, cable car, bicycle, tricycle, unicycle, wheelchair, skateboard; land, water, ground, people, city, lift, ski, mountain, fast, slowly, bumpy, move, travel, jump, people-powered, motor-powered*

Materials: Pictures to represent the vocabulary above; old magazines, scissors, glue, sheets of paper, pencils and crayons.

Learner's Book

 Warm up

- Revise the poem *My big blue boat* from **Lesson 4**.
- Ask confident learners to recite the poem on their own if they feel comfortable.

1 Before you read

- Open books at page 102. Focus on the questions. Elicit different means of transport from learners.
- Show your pictures to introduce the new vocabulary.

> **Answers**
> Learners' own answers.

2 Read and listen 70 [CD2 Track 17]

- Ask learners if they have ever travelled in any of the vehicles they can see in the pictures.
- Play the recording once. Learners listen and follow in their books.
- Explain any vocabulary as necessary and play the recording again.

> **Audioscript:** Track 70
> See Learner's Book pages 102–104.

> **Answers**
> Learners' own answers.

AB **For further practice, see Activity 1 in the Activity Book.**

3 Make a chart

- Ask learners what they think *people-powered* and *motor-powered* mean.
- Ask them to look at the vehicles in the text and say which are people-powered and which are motor-powered.
- Elicit more vehicles from learners to include in each category.
- **Critical thinking:** Remind learners that a chart is used to classify information into categories according to a rule. In this chart, there are two categories. Elicit from learners different types of information they can classify using a similar chart to this, e.g. animals according to their number of legs, what they eat.

> **Answers**
> People-powered vehicles: bicycle, tricycle, unicycle, wheelchair, skateboard, skis, zorb
> Motor-powered vehicles: underground train, hydrofoil, lift, cable car

AB **For further practice, see Activities 2 and 3 and the Challenge in the Activity Book.**

Words to remember

- Write on the board the words: *go, can, up* and *down*.
- Learners look for the sight words in the text. How many times do they see the word? Tell them to count on their fingers.
- You could ask learners to make word cards for these words.
- Magazine hunt: Ask learners to look through old magazines and cut out letters to make sight words in their notebooks or on file cards.

> **Answers**
> *go* appears 8 times
> *can* appears 11 times
> *up* appears 3 times
> *down* appears 5 times

Language detective

- **Critical thinking:** Explain that there are parts of words that help us understand their meaning. We sometimes add these parts to existing words to make new ones.
- Focus on the list of prefixes and explain their meaning.
- Focus on the first question and elicit answers from the class. Elicit another word they know beginning with *tri-*.

> **Answers**
> *Tricycle* means a cycle with three wheels.
> The other word learners know beginning with *tri-* is *triangle*.

4 📝 My favourite vehicle

- Give learners a sheet of paper, pencils and crayons. They then draw their favourite vehicle.
- When they have finished, they show and describe it to the class.
- They then write a sentence about it following the model.

> **Answers**
> Learners' own answers.

 Warm up

- Ask the class to look at the pictures and say which vehicle they like most, which they have travelled by and which is the strangest.

Activity Book

1 Name the vehicle

- Focus on the pictures and elicit the names of the vehicles from learners. They then unscramble the letters to spell each word correctly.
- Check the answers by asking learners to take turns spelling and writing the words on the board.

- Then ask learners to circle the vehicles they have travelled in.

> **Answers**
> **1** skis **2** bus **3** cable car
> **4** lift **5** wheelchair **6** bicycle
> **7** train **8** plane

2 Make a chart

- Ask learners to look at the pictures and classify the vehicles into the two categories in the chart. They then write their answers in the chart.

> **Answers**
> People-powered vehicles: bicycle, tricycle, unicycle, wheelchair, skateboard, skis, zorb
> Motor-powered vehicles: underground train, hydrofoil, lift, cable car

Challenge

- Learners think of and add three more vehicles to the chart.

> **Suggested answers**
> Boat, motorbike, bus, car

3 Is it true?

- Ask learners to read the text in the Learner's Book again. Then they read the sentences and choose the right answer.
- Check answers as a class.

> **Answers**
> **1** yes **2** no **3** no
> **4** yes **5** yes **6** yes

I can talk about different vehicles and how they move.

- Direct learners' attention to the self-evaluation question at the top of page 84. Ask them to think and answer. Emphasise the importance of giving an honest answer.

> **Answers**
> Learners' own answers.

Differentiated instruction

Additional support and practice

- Ask learners to cut out letters and make illustrated word cards for the words beginning with the suffixes they have learnt.

Extend and challenge

- Ask learners to make another chart using different categories of transport, e.g. water vehicles and land vehicles.

Lesson 6: Choose a project

How do we travel around

Learner's Book pages: 106–107
Activity Book pages: 86–87

Lesson objectives

Listening: Listen to comprehension items in the Activity Book quiz.

Speaking: Present your project to the class, ask and answer questions about travel.

Reading: Read instructions, read a poem, read sentences to do a matching exercise in the Activity Book quiz.

Writing: Write a travel survey, write in a word flip book, write a poem, write words in the Activity Book quiz.

Language focus: Unit 7 Review

Materials:

A Do a travel survey: One sheet of paper for each learner, pencils and crayons, old magazines, glue, scissors.

B Make a word flip book: Different coloured card, scissors, glue, pencils and crayons, sheets of paper of different sizes.

C Make up your own version of a poem: Sheets of paper, pencils and crayons.

Learner's Book

☞ Warm up

- Play a guessing game: divide the class into two groups. Each group takes turns to mime an action they have learned in this unit. The other group guesses the word. Give the groups a point for each correct guess.

Choose a project

- Learners choose an end-of-unit project to work on. Look at the learner-made samples and help them choose. Move the children into groups depending on their choices. Provide materials.

A Do a travel survey
- Show the example survey in the Learner's Book.
- Give learners the pencils and crayons and cards to make their own chart. They may also use old magazines and cut out pictures to decorate it.
- They circulate asking their classmates the questions and recording the answers in the chart.
- They then report their findings to the class.

B Make a word flip book
- Read the instructions with the learners. Give them sheets of paper, pencils and crayons to make their book.
- When they have finished, they show their book to their friends and describe it.

C Make up your own version of a poem
- Read the poem with the learners. Help them with any new vocabulary.
- They choose a flying machine from the options they like and answer the questions.
- They then change the words to write their own description of a flying machine.
- They write their poem on a sheet of paper and draw a picture to accompany it.
- **Informal assessment opportunity:** Circulate as learners work. Informally assess their receptive and productive language skills. Check for correct pronunciation and spelling of new vocabulary. Ask questions. You may want to take notes on their responses.
- If possible, leave the learner projects on display for a short while, then consider filing the projects, photos or scans of the work, in learners' portfolios. Write the date on the work.

Look what I can do!
- Review the *I can ...* statements. Learners demonstrate what they can do.

Answer
teeth

 For further practice, see the quiz in the Activity Book.

Answers	
1 a	**4** a
2 b	**5** b
3 b	

Read and write
- For items 6 to 9, learners match the words to the pictures. Demonstrate by tracing with your finger.

Answers	
6 Picture c	**8** Picture b
7 Picture d	**9** Picture a

Activity Book

Unit 7 Quiz: Look what I can do!

Listen 97 [CD2 Track 44]
- For items 1 to 5, learners listen to the audio and tick the correct picture. Do the first item as a class. Play the audio several times.

Audioscript: Track 97

Narrator: 1

Speaker: I can slide down a slide.

Narrator: 2

Speaker: I can ride in an underground train.

Narrator: 3

Speaker: Wheelchairs with three wheels can go fast.

Narrator: 4

Speaker 1: How do you like travelling?

Speaker 2: I like travelling in a big black helicopter.

Narrator: 5

Speaker 1: How does she go to school?

Speaker 2: She goes by hydrofoil.

8 Wonderful water

Unit overview

In this unit learners will:
- Discuss the importance of water in their lives
- Talk about the weather
- Describe vehicles of different kinds
- Do a survey and describe results
- Write a poem
- Do an experiment and draw conclusions.

Learners will build communication and literacy skills as they speak about the importance of water for life, talk about things that float, discuss and act out a playscript, read a story and write a poem.

At the end of the unit, they will apply and personalise what they have learned by working in small groups to complete a project of their choice: doing a class survey, making a water mural, or doing an experiment.

Language focus

What's the weather like?

Present simple statements: *We all need water*

Present simple questions: *Wh-* and *Yes/No* questions

Vocabulary topics: Days of the week, weather words, verbs associated with weather conditions

Critical thinking
- Provide examples to support an idea
- Discuss information
- Classify into categories
- Do a survey and interpret results
- Do an experiment.

Self-assessment
- I can talk about the weather.
- I can say why plants, animals and people need water.
- I can ask and answer questions about which things float.
- I can read and write words with long **a** spellings **ay** and **ai**.

Teaching tips

Some of the words may be especially difficult for learners to pronounce, e.g. *Wednesday, Thursday.* Model the pronunciation and invite learners to repeat the days of the week several times to practise pronunciation.

Review the learner's work on the Activity Book quiz, noting areas where they demonstrate strength and areas where they need additional instruction and practice. Use this information to customise your teaching as you continue to **Unit 9**.

Lesson 1: Think about it

Why is water important?

Learner's Book pages: 108–109

Activity Book pages: 88–89

Lesson objectives

Listening: Listen to a poem, listen for information.

Speaking: Speak about the weather on each day of the week, practise theme vocabulary, ask and answer questions about daily activities.

Reading: Read a poem, discover missing words.

Writing: Write a poem.

Critical thinking: Discuss an issue and analyse consequences, memorise and recite a poem, write a poem following a model.

Language focus: Present simple questions: *What's the weather like? What do you do on (Sunday)?*

Vocabulary: Days of the week; different types of weather: *rainy, windy, cloudy, sunny, hot, warm, cold; umbrella, grass, tree, house, rain, flowers, puddle, boots, rain coat, tidy*

Materials: Real objects or pictures to represent the vocabulary above; pencils and crayons, card, scissors, sheets of A3 paper.

Learner's Book

Why is water important?

☞ Warm up

- Ask learners which poem or rhyme they like most from **Units 1** to **7** of the Learner's Book. Invite them to recite it in front of the class, or in groups for less confident learners.

Think about it

- Ask learners if they think water is important and why. What do they use water for? How much water do they drink during they day?
- Elicit answers from learners and provide English equivalents as necessary.
- **Critical thinking:** Invite learners to reflect on how much water/rain there is in their region. Is there enough? Too little? Too much? What might happen if there wasn't any water, or there was more?

☞ Introduce new vocabulary

- Show learners your pictures to introduce *rainy, windy, cloudy, sunny, hot, warm, cold, umbrella, grass, tree, house, rain, flowers, puddle, boots* and *rain coat*.
- Hold up each picture, say the word and ask learners to mime and repeat after you. Ask additional

questions, e.g. *What colour is the raincoat? Is the grass blue or green?*
- Show a calendar and introduce the days of the week to learners. Say: *The (first) day of the week is (Monday).*

1 Read and listen 71 [CD2 Track 18]

- Open books at page 108. Tell learners you are going to listen to a poem. Play the audio a few times.
- Play the poem again. Pause after each line for learners to repeat.
- Practise reciting the poem together.
- **Critical thinking:** Encourage learners to memorise and recite the poem using mime to help them remember key words.

> **Audioscript:** Track 71
>
> **Speaker:** *Rainy day*
>
> Rain on the green grass.
>
> Rain on the tree.
>
> Rain on the houses
>
> But not on me!

2 What can you see? 72 [CD2 Track 19]

- Focus on the picture. Tell learners that you are going to listen to a teacher and her class talking about what they can see through the window of the classroom.
- Play the audio a few times. Learners look at the pictures and point to what they hear as they listen.
- Play the audio again and pause after each line for learners to repeat.
- Ask questions about the picture, e.g. *What day is it? What's the weather like? What can the girl see? What are the people wearing?*
- **Personalisation:** Ask learners to look out of their own classroom window. Ask questions about what they can see and what the weather is like. This will provide an extra opportunity to recycle vocabulary and relate the use of English to their everyday life.

> **Audioscript:** Track 72
>
> **Teacher:** Today is Monday. It's windy and rainy.
>
> **Girl:** I can see people with umbrellas. The wind is blowing the umbrellas.
>
> **Teacher:** I can see people with coats and hats.
>
> **Girl:** I can see a little boy with a yellow raincoat, a yellow rain hat, and red boots. He likes the rain! He's jumping in a puddle.
>
> **Teacher:** I can see green grass and flowers and a tree. The grass, the flowers and the tree like the rain, too. They need rain to grow.

> **Suggested answers**
> Rain, people with umbrellas, wind blowing the umbrellas, coats and hats, a little boy in a yellow raincoat, a yellow rain hat and red boots, jumping in a puddle, green grass, flowers and a tree.

3 Topic vocabulary 73 [CD2 Track 20]

- Focus on page 109. Direct learners' attention to the words. Play the audio and mime to make the meanings clear.
- Play the audio again. Pause after each word so that learners can point to the correct picture and repeat.
- Write the words on the board. Read the words together. Check for correct pronunciation.
- Ask learners what kind of weather they like. Do they like rainy/cold/hot days?

Audioscript: Track 73
Speaker:

cloudy	It's a cloudy day. There are grey clouds in the sky.
windy	It's a windy day. Listen to the wind!
rainy	It's a rainy day. Listen to the rain!
sunny	It's a sunny day. Look at the sun in the sky.
snowy	It's a snowy day. Let's make a snowman!
hot	It's hot! Drink lots of water!
cold	Brrrrr … It's cold! Put on a jacket.

[AB] **For further practice, see Activity 1 in the Activity Book.**

4 What's the weather like?

- Learners look at the pictures and decide which word is missing from the sentences.
- They write the complete sentences in their notebook. Read the sentences together as a class.

Answers
It is hot and **sunny**.
It is cold and **snowy**.

5 Days of the week 74 [CD2 Track 21]

- Ask learners what they do on different days of the week. Remind them of activities they have studied previously in the book. Elicit a few answers.
- Focus on the pictures and the phrases. Tell learners that they are going to listen to the chant and mime.
- Play the audio a few times while learners chant along.
- Ask questions: *What do you do on (Monday)?* Learners then practise the questions with a partner.

Audioscript: Track 74
Speaker: <u>Mon</u>day, <u>Tues</u>day, <u>Wed</u>nesday, <u>Thurs</u>day, <u>Fri</u>day, <u>Sat</u>urday, <u>Sun</u>day.

On Monday, I read a book
I read a book, I read a book.
On Tuesday, I sing a song,
I sing a song on Tuesday.
On Wednesday, I write a poem,
I write a poem, I write a poem.

On Thursday, I fly a kite,
I fly a kite on Thursday.
On Friday, I drive a car,
I drive a car, I drive a car.
On Saturday, I tidy my room,
I tidy my room on Saturday.
On Sunday, I feed my cat,
I feed my cat, I feed my cat,
On Sunday, I feed my cat,
Meow, meow, meow!

Answers
Learners' own answers.

[AB] **For further practice, see Activities 2 and 3 in the Activity Book.**

6 Keep a weather journal

- Ask learners to keep their own weather journal for a week. They write: *Today is_____. It is _____.*
- Encourage them to add a drawing and a personal comment or observation to the journal entry.

Wrap up

- **Home–school link:** Learners recite the poem and the chant to the family.

Activity Book

1 What's the weather like?

- Direct learners' attention to the pictures, mime the weather types. Learners then work independently to unscramble the letters and write the words correctly.
- When they have finished, ask learners to take turns spelling the words. They could also write them on the board.

Answers
1 windy
2 rainy
3 sunny
4 snowy

2 Days of the week

- Read the first instruction and elicit answers from the class. Ask learners to write the answers in their Activity Book.
- Read the other questions. Learners work independently. Check answers as a class. Ask more confident learners to read out their own sentences.

3 Write a rainy day poem

- Ask learners to read the poem on page 108 of the Learner's Book.
- Write the poem on the board.
- Underline the words which they can change (*green grass*, *houses*).
- Elicit ideas for replacement words.
- Tell learners to study the **Word box**. They then use words from the box to complete the sentences to make a poem. Learners draw a picture of their poem.

I can talk about the weather.

- Direct learners' attention to the self-evaluation question at the top of page 88. Ask them to think and answer. Emphasise the importance of giving an honest answer.

Differentiated instruction
Extend and challenge

- 💬 Ask learners to create a new chant using the one in the Learner's Book on page 108 as a model. Invite them to revisit previous units and use vocabulary they have learnt.

Lesson 2: Find out more

Facts about water
Learner's Book pages: 110–111
Activity Book pages: 90–91

Lesson objectives

Listening: Listen to and understand key information, listen to and follow instructions.

Speaking: Practise science vocabulary, discuss information.

Reading: Read and understand factual information, read and understand instructions.

Writing: Complete sentences using information.

Critical thinking: Provide examples to support an idea, classify things into categories.

Writing tip: Use capital letters and full stops.

Language focus: Present simple: statements and questions: *Animals need water to drink. What do plants need to grow?*

Vocabulary: *living things, rain, snow, river, lake, rock;* animals: *frog, turtle, crocodile, whale;* verbs: *live, need, grow, drink, dry, wash, make*

Materials: Pictures to represent the vocabulary above, pictures of deserts (or very dry landscapes) and jungles (or places where water is plentiful), pencils and crayons, card, scissors, poster paper.

Learner's Book

🖙 Warm up

- Ask learners: *What's the weather like today? Is it rainy or sunny?*
- Elicit answers from the class. They then write in their weather journal and draw a picture.
- As a class, chant the days of the week together.

🖙 Introduce vocabulary

- Introduce key vocabulary: *frog, turtle, crocodile, whale.* Show learners the pictures and say the words. Learners repeat.
- Then introduce the concept of *living things.* Say: *A (turtle) is a living thing, a (plant) is a living thing. Is a (rock) a living thing?* Elicit more examples from learners.

1 🖾 Before you read

- Open books at page 110. Show the pictures of dry and wet places and ask: *What do plants need to grow? What do animals need to grow?* Invite learners to share their answers.
- Point to the pictures and ask: *What is the same about rain, snow, rivers and lakes?*
- Explain that in many places there is a *dry season* and a *rainy season*. In the dry season, there is no rain. In the rainy season, there is a lot of rain. Which picture on the page shows the dry season? How do they know?
- Supply additional vocabulary as necessary.
- **Critical thinking:** Ask learners to discuss in pairs what they see in the pictures and draw conclusions from them. Ask: *Are there plants in picture? What happens with the animals in this picture?*

🔲 **For further practice, see Activities 1 and 2 in the Activity Book.**

2 Read and listen 🔾75 [CD2 Track 22]

- Point to the pictures and revise the vocabulary.
- Play the audio a few times. Learners follow in their books.
- You may wish to ask more confident learners to read a sentence each along with the audio script or after learners have finished listening.

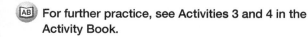 For further practice, see Activities 3 and 4 in the Activity Book.

3 Animals that live in water

- Ask learners to look at the pictures on page 111 and name the animals.
- Then ask: *Does a fish live in water? Can a turtle live on land?* Learners answer. Elicit the differences between an animal that can only live in water, amphibians, and animals that can only live on land.
- Make a list on the board of the animals that live in water. Add more examples.
- **Critical thinking:** You could ask learners to make a table on the board and classify the animals. Encourage them to provide more categories, e.g. water, land, both. They could then add more examples to each category.

> **Answers**
> Frogs, fish, turtles, crocodiles and whales live in water.
> Other animals that live in water are octopuses, sharks, seals, shellfish.

4 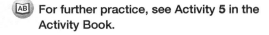 Write about it

- Explain the activity. Model first with one animal of your choice.
- Learners then proceed independently and write their sentences in their notebooks. They illustrate each sentence with a picture.
- Invite a few learners to read their sentences to the class.

> **Answers**
> Learners' own answers.

Writing tip

- Remind learners of the use of capital letters at the beginning of a sentence and full stop at the end. Ask them to find other examples of this in the lesson.

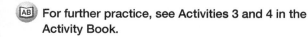 For further practice, see Activity 5 in the Activity Book.

5 How we use water

- Focus on the pictures and read the sentences together.
- Invite learners to discuss other ways in which we use water. Provide additional vocabulary as necessary.

> **Suggested answers**
> We use water to wash cars.
> We use water to clean the floor.
> We use water to play with.
> We use water to take a shower.

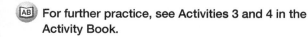 For further practice, see Activity 6 in the Activity Book.

6 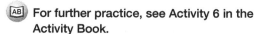 Make a class book

- Remind learners of the different ways we use water from **Activity 5**.
- Learners write a sentence and draw a picture to make a page in the class book.

Wrap up

- Challenge the class to think of as many uses for water as possible. You may set a time limit to make the activity more exciting.

Activity Book

1 Living things

- Focus on the pictures and elicit the words from the learners. They circle the correct pictures. Check answers as a class.

> **Answers**
> *Turtle, apple tree, rabbit*

2 Draw and write

- After learners have finished **Activity 1**, ask them to draw two more living things and write the words on the lines provided.
- Ask individual learners what living things they have written and drawn about.

> **Answers**
> Learners' own answers.

3 Watery words!

- Remind learners what a word snake is and ask them to find the words in it. They then circle the words next to the correct picture.

> **Answers**
> asrainghtsnowprdrinknidfwaterfgglaketyriverza

4 Label the picture

- Focus on the picture and ask learners to label it with the correct words. Ask learners to show their work to the class when they have finished.

> **Answers**
> 1 snow
> 2 rain
> 3 river
> 4 lake

5 Over to you

- Talk with learners about their own region. Is there a lot of water, or not enough? Remind them of the discussion at the beginning of the lesson.
- Focus on the questions. Read them aloud and ask them to write their answers. Circulate, helping with spelling as necessary.

> **Answers**
> Learners' own answers.

6 How do we use water?

- Focus on the pictures. Ask learners to complete the sentences using the words and pictures from the box to help them. Check answers as a class.

> **Answers**
> 1 clothes
> 2 tea

I can say why plants, animals and people need water.

- Direct learners' attention to the self-evaluation question at the top of page 90. Ask them to think and answer. Emphasise the importance of giving an honest answer.

> **Answers**
> Learners' own answers.

> ### Differentiated instruction
>
> **Additional support and practice**
>
> - Ask learners to make word cards for key vocabulary. They choose two or three words and make illustrated word cards.
>
> **Extend and challenge**
>
> - 🖳 Learners make a new table with headings of the following categories: *sea, river, land.* They think of animals that live in each type of environment, fill the table and make a mini poster.

Lesson 3: Letters and sounds

Long *a* spellings *ai* and *ay*

Learner's Book pages: 112–113
Activity Book pages: 92–93

> ### Lesson objectives
>
> **Listening:** Listen to a poem and a story, identify the sound of long *a* spellings *ai* and *ay.*
>
> **Speaking:** Say a poem, act out a story.
>
> **Reading:** Recognise words with long **a**, read and follow instructions, read a story and answer questions about it.
>
> **Writing:** Complete sentences, write rhyming words.
>
> **Critical thinking:** Memorise and recite a story, listen to and recite a poem, identify characters in a story.

> **Language focus:** Blending long **a** words
> **Vocabulary:** *go away, day, stay, snail*

> **Materials:** Pictures or word cards to represent the vocabulary above.

Learner's Book

🖙 Warm up

- Ask learners: *What's the weather like today? Is it rainy or sunny?*
- Elicit answers from the class. Then they write in their weather journal and draw a picture of the weather.
- Write a few words with different short sounds the class has learned so far and ask learners to find pairs of words that rhyme.

1 Rain poem 76 [CD2 Track 23]

- Learners open books at page 112. Point to the poem and say: *Let's listen.*
- Play the audio twice. Then focus on the words in the poem. Ask learners what sounds they make.
- Ask them to find all the words that have the same sound. Check as a class.

> **Audioscript:** Track 76
> **Speaker:** Rain, rain, go away.
>
>   Come again some other day.
>
>   All the children want to play.

> **Answers**
> *Rain, away, again, day, play*

2 Mystery word

- Read the instructions and explain the activity.
- Learners work in pairs and complete the words. When they have finished, check their answers as a class.

> **Answers**
> **1** It's a rainy day.
> **2** Let's paint a snail.
> **3** Let's play with the train.

 For further practice, see Activities 1, 2 and 3 and the **Challenge** in the Activity Book.

3 Phonics story 77 [CD2 Track 24]

- Direct learners' attention to the pictures. Ask: *What can you see in the pictures? What's the weather like? Let's listen.*
- Play the audio once. Point at each picture to help learners understand.
- Play the audio again. Pause after each line for learners to repeat and mime.
- Tell learners to listen again and put up their hands when they hear words with the long **a** sound.
- Ask them to write the words in their notebooks.
- Invite learners to point at the pictures and read the story along with the recording.

> **Audioscript:** Track 77
> **Speaker:** *Please stay and play*
>
> It's a rainy day. Little Snail is playing with the frogs and the ducks.
>
> 'Good-bye, Little Snail,' the little frogs say.
>
> 'Wait, wait! Don't go. Please stay and play.'
>
> 'Sorry, Little Snail. We need to go away.'
>
> 'Good-bye, Little Snail,' the white ducks say.
>
> 'Wait, wait! Don't go. Please stay and play.'
>
> 'Sorry, Little Snail. We need to go away.'
>
> 'Hello, Little Snail,' the big snails say.
>
> 'Hello, big snails! Please stay and play.'
>
> 'Sure, Little Snail. We can play all day.'
>
> 'Hooray!'

> **Answers**
> *Stay, play, rainy, day, Snail, playing, say, wait, away, hooray.*

4 Act it out

- **Critical thinking:** Remind learners of what a character is and ask them to find the characters in the story.
- Elicit who the characters are and make a list on the board.
- Divide the class into groups and ask learners to choose a role from the story.
- Learners then act out the story.

Wrap up

- Ask learners to choose a line of the phonics story and recite it as quickly as they can.
- **Home–school link:** Learners recite and teach the poem and the story to the family. They can also act out the story with parents and siblings.

Activity Book

1 Read and draw

- Read the sentences as a class. Point to the pictures and elicit the answers. Ask learners to circle the correct words and then follow the instructions to colour the picture.

> **Answers**
> *-ai words: painting, paint, sail, snail*
> *-ay words: day, playing*

2 Rhyming words

- Remind learners of rhyming words from the beginning of the lesson. Focus on the pictures and the words and say them together.
- Ask learners to write the missing words. Check as a class.

> **Answers**
> **1** *Sail/snail*
> **2** *Rain/train*
> **3** *Say/play*

3 Make a sentence

- Ask learners to choose a word from the previous exercise and write a sentence about it, then draw a picture to match.
- When they have finished, ask them to read their sentences out to the class.

> **Answers**
> Learners' own answers.

Challenge

- Now ask learners to choose two words and write a sentence using both of them. When they have finished, ask them to read their sentence in turn.

> **Answers**
> Learners' own answers.

I can read and write words with long *a* spellings *ay* and *ai*.

- Direct learners' attention to the self-evaluation question at the top of page 92. Ask them to think and answer. Emphasise the importance of giving an honest answer.

> **Answers**
> Learners' own answers.

Differentiated instruction

Additional support and practice

- Learners write words they remember that contain the long **a**. They can also draw pictures to represent the words.

Extend and challenge

- Pass out paper and pencils. Learners write their name at the top of the paper, then create a tongue twister using words from this lesson. Collect their work, write the date on the back, and save in the learners' portfolio.

Lesson 4: Use of English

Things that float

Learner's Book pages: 114–115
Activity Book pages: 94–95

> ### Lesson objectives
>
> **Speaking:** Discuss things that float, act out a conversation.
>
> **Reading:** Read and complete sentences, follow instructions.
>
> **Writing:** Complete sentences, answer questions.
>
> **Critical thinking:** Make an experiment, observe and compare things, draw conclusions, classify things.
>
> **Writing tip:** Join **do + not** to make **don't**, and **does + not** to make **doesn't**.

> **Language focus:** Present simple affirmative and negative statements: *A boat floats, A coin doesn't float.*
>
> Questions: *Does a coin float?*
>
> **Vocabulary:** *Coin, pear, float, elastic band, paper clip, row, down the stream, dream, scream, shiver, polar bear, crocodile, lion, waterfall, shore, river*

> **Materials:** Pictures or word cards to represent the vocabulary above; a bowl of water, pencils and crayons, pieces of A4 paper, map of the world.

Learner's Book

Warm up

- Ask learners: *What's the weather like today? Is it rainy or sunny?*
- Elicit answers from the class. Then they write in their weather journal and draw a picture.
- In groups, learners act out the story in **Lesson 3**.

Introduce new vocabulary

- Show your pictures in turn and say the new words. Learners listen and repeat.
- Show the pictures in random order and have learners say the words without prompting, then write them on the board.

1 Does it float?

- Look at the picture and read the questions to the learners. Discuss the answers as a class.
- Learners copy the sentences in their notebooks and draw a picture for each sentences.
- **Critical thinking:** Encourage learners to observe and discuss why some things float and some don't. This will be useful preparation for the next activity.

> **Answers**
> 1 The apple floats.
> 2 The paper clip doesn't float.
> 3 The pear doesn't float.
> 4 The paper boat floats.

2 Let's find out

- Give each pair the objects to carry out the experiments.
- Following the model in the book, ask the class about the pencil. Carry out the experiment as a class.
- In pairs, learners discuss the other items using the model in the book, and then proceed to test their ideas and record their results.

> **Suggested answers**
> The pencil, paper and leaf float.
> The elastic band, ruler and paper clip don't float.

> [AB] For further practice, see Activities 1 and 2 in the Activity Book.

3 🎵 Floating in a boat 78 [CD2 Track 25]

- Focus on the picture and introduce any new vocabulary using the picture cards. Ask learners where lions, polar bears and crocodiles live. Have they ever seen these animals?
- Tell learners you are going to listen to a song. Play the audio. Learners follow in their books.
- Play the audio a few times. As learners grow more confident, they mime along as they listen.
- Play the audio again. Pause after each verse for learners to repeat.

Audioscript: Track 78

Speaker: *Row, row, row your boat*

Row, row, row your boat
Gently down the stream.
Merrily, merrily, merrily, merrily,
Life is but a dream.

Row, row, row your boat,
Gently down the stream.
If you see a crocodile,
Don't forget to scream!

Row, row, row your boat,
Gently down the river.
If you see a polar bear,
Don't forget to shiver!

Row, row, row your boat,
Gently float about.
If you see a waterfall,
Don't forget to shout!

Row, row, row your boat,
Gently to the shore.
If you see a lion,
Don't forget to roar!

Row, row, row your boat,
Gently in the bath.
If you see a spider,
Don't forget to laugh!

Row, row, row your boat,
Gently down the stream.
Merrily, merrily, merrily, merrily,
Life is a but a dream.

4 💬 Don't forget! 79 [CD2 Track 26]

- Tell learners that you are going to listen to a conversation between a mother and her daughter.
- Play the conversation a few times. Pause after each exchange for learners to repeat.
- As they grow more confident, encourage them to practise the conversation in pairs from memory.

Audioscript: Track 79

Girl: Mum, I'm going out to play.

Mum: Don't forget your boots!

Girl: Yes, Mum.

Mum: Don't forget your raincoat.

Girl: Yes, Mum.

Mum: Don't forget your umbrella.

Girl: OK, I'm going now.

Mum: Bye. And don't forget to have fun!

Girl: Bye, Mum!

[AB] **For further practice, see Activity 3 in the Activity Book.**

📣 Wrap up

- Learners work in pairs and create a new conversation, changing the weather and the objects in the model audio. Then they act it out.
- **Home–school link:** Learners teach the song *Row your boat* to the family. They can also carry out the experiment together with different objects. Then they record the results. Learners can tell the class what they have done.

Activity Book

1 Does it float?

- When learners have finished **Activity 1** in the Learner's Book, ask them to record the results in the table in the Activity Book. Check the results of the chart as a class.

Suggested answers
Pencil: yes
Paper: yes
Elastic band: no
Ruler: no
Paper clip: no
Leaf: yes

Writing tip

- Ask learners to find the words *doesn't* and *don't* in the texts. Explain how they are created by joining the words *does + not* and *do + not*.

2 Write about it

- Tell learners to write sentences about their results. Circulate, giving help with spelling if necessary.

Answers
Learners' own answers.

3 Don't forget!

- Focus on the picture. Remind learners of the conversation and ask them to write down what the girl has forgotten.

- Then, they write the sentence. Check answers as a class. Learners could also colour in the picture.

> **Answers**
> Learners' own answers.

I can ask and answer questions about which things float.

- Direct learners' attention to the self-evaluation question at the top of page 94. Ask them to think and answer. Emphasise the importance of giving an honest answer.

> **Answers**
> Learners' own answers.

Differentiated instruction

Additional support and practice

- Learners collect objects and experiment with them using a bowl of water. Do they float? They draw the pictures and record their findings in a mini poster.

Extend and challenge

- Learners look for information about where lions, crocodiles and polar bears live. They make word cards with the name of the animals on them and place them on a map of the world. They can also look for and name important rivers (the Nile, the Amazon) and waterfalls (Victoria, Iguazú, Niagara) on the map.

Lesson 5: Read and respond

Learner's Book pages: 116–119
Activity Book pages: 96–97

Lesson objectives

Listening: Listen to a traditional story.

Speaking: Make predictions about a story, discuss the plot, act out the story.

Reading: Read along as you listen, do a reading comprehension exercise, practise sight words.

Writing: Write sentences and add exclamation marks to sentences.

Critical thinking: Understand the correct sequence of a story, make predictions, make inferences, recall information, assess characters.

Writing tip: Use exclamation marks.

Language focus: The verb *need*: *We need water*, revision of *Let's*: *Let's go to the Emperor in the Clouds*, revision of *there's*: *There's no food to eat*, revision of *can*: *You can sing*

Sight words: *need, we, come, no*

Vocabulary: *mud, food, eat, drink, Emperor, clouds, guard*; animals: *toad, bees, rooster, tiger*

Materials: Pictures or word cards to represent the vocabulary above; a map of the world or globe; glue, scissors, pencils and crayons, a copy of **Photocopiable activity 15** for each learner, coloured paper for the hats, old magazines.

Learner's Book

↪ Warm up

- Ask learners: *What's the weather like today? Is it rainy or sunny?*
- Elicit answers from the class. Then they write in their weather journal and draw a picture.
- Ask learners about their favourite stories in the Learner's Book so far. Invite them to say why they like them and who their favourite characters are.

1 Before you read 80 [CD2 Track 27]

- Focus on the pictures to introduce the characters.
- Ask: *Is this a song? Is it a poem? A story? Is it a play? Why?* Ask learners to explain the difference between the four options and say which they think this is.
- Read the title. Tell learners look at the pictures on page 116 and predict what the story will be about.
- Point out Vietnam on a world map or globe. Help learners find their own country on the map/globe and with their finger trace the route from their country to Vietnam. Is anybody from Vietnam?
- Read the background to the story. Remind learners of what a dry season is.
- Play the recording once. Learners listen and follow in their books to check if they were right.
- Play the recording again. Ask questions to check comprehension of the story.

> **Audioscript:** Track 80
> See Learner's Book pages 116–118.

 For further practice, see Activity 1 in the Activity Book.

2 Characters

- Read questions. Learners look at the pictures and discuss in pairs or small groups.
- Elicit their opinions. They can write their answers in their notebooks.
- **Critical thinking:** Ask learners if they know any other stories where the main characters are animals.

> **Answers**
> The characters are: 1 Toad, 2 Bee, 3 Green Guard, 4 Purple Guard, 5 Emperor, 6 Rooster, 7 Tiger.
> The animal characters are: Toad, Rooster, Tiger, Bee.
> The animals need rain because there is no food to eat, there is no water to drink, and the flowers are dry (the bees need flowers to live).

Words to remember

- Write the words *need*, *we*, *come* and *no* on the board.
- Learners look for the sight words in the text. How many times do they see the word? Tell them to count on their fingers. They then read the sentence where the word appears.
- You may ask learners to make word cards for these words.
- Magazine hunt: Ask learners to look through old magazines and cut out letters to make sight words in their notebooks or on file cards.
- Review the following sight words from previous units: *you*, *go*, *to*. Ask learners to look for these words in the text of the play as well.

> **Answers**
> *need* appears 9 times
> *we* appears 5 times
> *come* appears 8 times
> *no* appears 5 times
> *you* appears 6 times (and once in the contraction *you're*)
> *go* appears 4 times
> *to* appears 7 times

3 Play questions

- Ask the questions in turn. Learners look back at the story and answer.
- You may wish to write the answers on the board and ask learners to copy them in their notebooks.
- **Critical thinking:** This activity requires learners to make decisions about the text, read the story again to look for the information they need and also make inferences about the feelings of the animals.

> **Answers**
> **1** in the clouds
> **2** to send rain
> **3** Yes, he does.
> **4** happy

4 Exclamation marks

- Explain what we use exclamation marks for. Learners read the sentences.
- Learners look for examples of exclamation mark use in the story.
- They then read the examples aloud, giving the sentences/phrases with exclamation marks the correct emphasis.

> **Answers**
> No!, Come, Bees!, Come, Rooster!, Help! Help!, There's a toad on my lap!, Come, Tiger!, ROAR!, It's raining!, Hooray for the rain!, Please don't come back!

 For further practice, see Activity **2** in the Activity Book.

5 Act it out

- Give each learner a copy of **Photocopiable activity 15** and pencils and crayons to colour the puppets.
- They also make hats for the Emperor and the Guards.
- When they have finished, divide class into five groups: Rooster, Tiger, the Bees, Toad, the Purple and Green Guards.
- Play the recording and pause to let the group playing that character repeat the line.
- Learners switch roles and repeat.

 For further practice, see Activity 3 in the Activity Book.

Wrap up

- Ask the class to choose their favourite character and mime it. The class guesses who it is. Then they say why they like it.
- **Home–school link:** Learners tell the story to their family. They could also look for more information about Vietnam together and make a poster at home to bring into class.

Activity Book

1 The song of the toad

- Focus on the pictures and read the questions with learners in turn. Explain to them that they have to order the pictures in the correct sequence.
- They work independently and then in pairs they discuss their decisions.
- Check the order of the pictures as a class.
- **Critical thinking:** Remind learners that stories follow a sequence, the order in which things happen, and this sequence is essential in understanding the plot.

> **Answers**
> Order of pictures: B1, D2, A3, C4, E5

2 What do the characters say?

- Focus on the pictures. Ask learners to complete the speech bubbles with the words they think the characters say in the play.
- When they have finished, check answers as a class.

> **Writing tip**
> - Focus on the **Writing tip** box and remind learners of what exclamation marks are for.

> **Answers**
> Learners' own answers.

3 Draw and write

- Ask learners to choose a scene they like from the play and draw it in the Activity Book.
- They then write what the characters say. Remind them to use exclamation marks, full stops, capital letters and question marks correctly in their writing.

> **Answers**
> Learners' own answers.

I can talk about the weather.

- Focus on the self-evaluation question at the top of page 96. Ask learners to think and answer. Emphasise the importance of giving an honest answer.

> **Answers**
> Learners' own answers.

> ### Differentiated instruction
>
> **Additional support and practice**
>
> - Ask learners to write some sentences with exclamation marks, using the dialogues in the play as a model. Then they exchange them with other learners and read them using the correct intonation.
>
> **Extend and challenge**
>
> - Ask learners to look for information about the animals of Vietnam. Then they make a poster and write the names of the animals – they can compare posters. They can also make illustrated word cards and place them on a map of Vietnam.

Lesson 6: Choose a project

Why is water important?

Learner's Book pages: 120–121

Activity Book pages: 98–99

> ### Lesson objectives / Assessment opportunities
>
> **Listening:** Listen to comprehension items in the Activity Book quiz.
>
> **Speaking:** Present your project to the class, ask questions for a survey, describe the results of a survey.
>
> **Reading:** Read instructions, read sentences to do a matching exercise in the Activity Book quiz.
>
> **Writing:** Do a weather survey, make a water world mural, record information in a chart, write words in the Activity Book quiz.

> **Language focus: Unit 8** Review

> **Materials:**
>
> **A Do a weather survey:** Sheets of paper to copy chart.
>
> **B Make a water world mural:** Pencils and crayons, A3 sheets of paper.
>
> **C Do an experiment: Does your boat float?** Sheets of paper, coins, sticky tape, a copy of **Photocopiable activity 16** for each learner, a bowl of water.

Warm up

- Ask learners: *What's the weather like today? Is it rainy or sunny?*
- Elicit answers from the class. Then they write in their weather journal and draw a picture.

Choose a project

- Learners choose an end-of-unit project to work on. Look at the learner-made samples and help them choose. Move the children into groups depending on their choices. Provide materials.

A Do a weather survey

- Read the instructions in the Learner's Book and show the example survey.
- Ask learners to copy the chart on a sheet of paper.
- Learners circulate, asking the questions and recording the answers in the survey.
- They then report the results of the survey to the class.

B Make a water world mural

- Give learners A3 sheets of paper, pencils and crayons.
- They draw their picture, including all the items indicated in the book.
- They then label the mural and show it to the class.

C Do an experiment: Does your boat float?

- Guide learners through the experiment instructions.
- Give each learner a copy of **Photocopiable activity 16**.
- They make their boats and do the experiment, putting more coins in the boat each time, recording the results in their chart. Note: Boats can be made from a wide variety of materials, for example recycled plastic lids, containers, aluminium foil, depending on what is available.
- Learners then make a different boat and repeat the experiment.
- Learners check the new results against the previous ones and report back to the class.
- **Informal assessment opportunity:** Circulate as learners work. Informally assess their receptive and productive language skills. Check for correct pronunciation and spelling of new vocabulary. Ask questions. You may want to take notes on their responses.
- If possible, leave the learner projects on display for a short while, then consider filing the projects, photos or scans of the work in learners' portfolios. Write the date on the work.

Look what I can do!

- Review the *I can …* statements. Learners demonstrate what they can do.

> **Answer**
> rainy day

 For further practice, see the quiz in the Activity Book.

Unit 8 Quiz: Look what I can do!

Listen 98 [CD2 Track 45]

- For items 1 to 5, learners listen to the audio and tick the correct picture. Do the first item as a class.
- Play the audio several times.

Audioscript: Track 98

Narrator: 1

Speaker: Today is Tuesday. It's sunny and hot.

Narrator: 2

Speaker: Plants need water to grow.

Narrator: 3

Speaker: Some animals live in water.

Narrator: 4

Speaker: The apple floats. The orange doesn't float.

Narrator: 5

Speaker: When there is no rain, the land becomes dry. Plants can't grow.

Answers
1 b
2 c
3 c
4 b
5 a

Read and write

- For items 6 and 7, learners tick the correct pictures. For items 8 and 9, learners write the words to go with the pictures.

Answers
6 a
7 b
8 rain
9 play

9 City places

Big question What can you see, hear and do in a city?

Unit overview

In this unit learners will:

- Speak about city sights and sounds
- Talk about traffic safety
- Describe parts of the city
- Ask for and give something
- Read, discuss and perform a poem
- Learn how to use a map.

Learners will build communication and literacy skills as they speak about city sights and sounds, talk about parts of the city, discuss and perform a poem, roleplay asking and giving something, play a game and sing a song.

At the end of the unit, they will apply and personalise what they have learned by working in small groups to complete a project of their choice: writing a poem, drawing a city map, or making an opposites book.

Language focus

Opposites

Determiners: *this/that*

Pronouns: *this/those*

Questions: *What's this? What are these?*

Vocabulary topics: City sights, buildings, traffic safety, locations, British and American English words

Critical thinking

- Classify information in a chart
- Understand the basic use of a map
- Discuss a poem
- Understand differences between languages.

Self-assessment

- I can name things in a city.
- I can name opposites.
- I can read and write words that end in **-y**.
- I can talk about things using *this* and *that*.

Teaching tip

Explain how to work with crosswords using definitions and visual clues. Learners have to pay attention to several things at the same time which might prove difficult at the beginning.

Lesson 1: Think about it

What can you see, hear and do in a city?

Learner's Book pages: 122–123

Activity Book pages: 100–101

Lesson objectives

Listening: Listen to a poem, count syllables.

Speaking: Speak about city sights and sounds, practise theme vocabulary, ask and answer questions.

Reading: Read a poem, read a text and draw.

Writing: Write a description about a city.

Critical thinking: Memorise and recite a poem.

Language focus: Revision of present continuous: *Paco is walking home.* Revision of present simple: *Red means STOP.* Revision of *can.*

Vocabulary: *city, stop, wait, go, road, shops, traffic, traffic lights, bus stop*

Materials: Pictures to represent the vocabulary above; pencils and crayons, card, scissors, poster paper; a copy of **Photocopiable activity 17** for each learner.

Learner's Book

Warm up

- Ask learners: *What's the weather like today? Is it rainy or sunny?*
- Elicit answers from the class. Then they write in their weather journal and draw a picture.

Think about it

- Do learners live in a city or in the countryside? Discuss what they can see in a city. Is it the same as in the countryside? What can they hear in the city? What about in the countryside? What about the smells? Are they the same?
- **Critical thinking:** Invite learners to compare what they think life is like in the city and in the countryside.

Introduce new vocabulary

- Show your pictures to introduce the vocabulary. Mime to introduce the verbs.
- Hold up each picture or mime, say the word and ask learners to mime and repeat after you.

1 Read and listen 81 [CD2 Track 28]

- Open books at page 122. Focus on the picture. Ask: *What can you see in the picture?* Elicit as many answers from learners as possible.
- Tell learners you are going to listen to a poem. Play the audio a few times.
- Play the poem again. Pause after each line for learners to repeat.

- Practise reciting the poem together.
- **Critical thinking:** Encourage learners to memorise and recite the poem using mime to help them remember.

Audioscript: Track 81

Speaker: *The traffic lights*

> Red means STOP.
>
> Green means GO.
>
> Yellow means WAIT,
>
> Even if you're late.

2 Walking in the city 82 [CD2 Track 29]

- Focus on the picture and ask questions, e.g. *What can we see in this picture? What are the child and his mother wearing? Can you see any vehicles? What shops can we see?*
- Tell learners to listen and follow Paco's route on the picture.
- Play the audio a few times. Learners look at the picture and follow as they listen.
- Play the audio again and pause after each line for learners to repeat.
- **Critical thinking:** Ask learners what maps are for. What kind of things can they usually see on a map?
- **Personalisation:** Ask learners about what they see on their way to school. This will provide an extra opportunity to practise vocabulary and relate the use of English to their everyday life.

Audioscript: Track 82

Boy: We live in a city. Every afternoon, my mum meets me at my school. My school is on a busy road. There are lots of cars and buses. Listen to the traffic! It's very noisy. We wait for the traffic to stop. We look left. We look right. Then my mum and I cross the road.

We walk on the pavement. We look at the shops. Mmm. I can smell bread.

It smells nice!

We go into the bakery.

Baker: Good afternoon. How are you?

Mum: Fine, thank you. We'd like some bread, please.

Baker: Big or small?

Mum: Big, please.

Baker: Here you are!

Boy: We leave the bakery. I'm carrying the bread. Can you see us? I'm wearing a red jacket and my mum is wearing a yellow dress. We cross the road again. We're walking to our bus stop. Can you see it? Here comes our bus! My mum and I get on the bus and ride home.

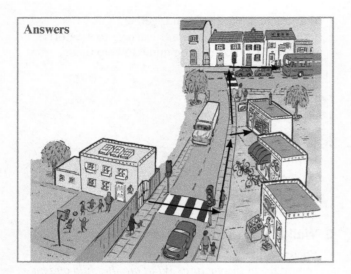

Answers

3 Topic vocabulary 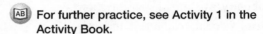 83 [CD2 Track 30]

- Focus on page 123. Direct learners' attention to the words. Play the audio and make the meanings clear.
- Play the audio again. Pause after each word and sentence for learners to repeat.
- Write the key words on the board. Read the words together. Check for correct pronunciation.
- Tell learners to listen again and clap the syllables.
- Play the audio again. Learners count the syllables.

Answers
City: two syllables
Road: one syllable
Pavement: two syllables
Shops: one syllable
Traffic: two syllables
Traffic light: three syllables
Bus stop: two syllables

Audioscript: Track 83
Speaker: city
  road
  pavement
  shops
  traffic
  traffic light
  bus stop
  cit-y
  road
  pave-ment
  shops
  traff-ic
  traff-ic light
  bus stop

4 Spot the word 82 [CD2 Track 29]

- Tell learners to look back at the big picture on page 122.
- Tell them to listen again to the audio and put up their hands when they hear a topic vocabulary word.

5 Questions

- Ask learners to look at the big picture again.
- Ask learners to answer the questions. Check their answers as a class.

Answers
1 Learners point to the big green bus.
2 There are three shops.
3 They stop and wait.

[AB] For further practice, see Activity 1 in the Activity Book.

6 Play the game '*Traffic lights*'

- Explain the rules of the game.
- At the start of each game, ask learners to move in different ways: hop like a rabbit, walk on your toes, etc.
- Play a few rounds.

7 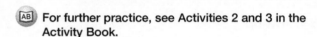 Write and draw

- Ask the questions in turn. Elicit answers from learners and make a list on the board of their ideas.
- Ask learners to write the answers in their Activity Book.

Answers
Learners' own answers.

[AB] For further practice, see Activities 2 and 3 in the Activity Book.

Wrap up

- Ask the class to recite and mime the poem 'The Traffic Lights'.
- **Home–school link:** Learners recite the poem and the chant to their family.

Activity Book

1 Read, draw and colour

- Ask learners to read the instructions. Then they draw and colour the picture.
- When they have finished, they show their work to the class and describe it.

Answers
Learners' own answers.

2 What can you hear and see in a city?

- Ask learners to classify in the table what they can hear and see in the city. Tell them to look at page 143 in the **Picture dictionary** for help if they need any ideas.
- When they have finished, check answers as a class.

Answers
Learners' own answers.

3 Write and draw

- Ask learners to write two sentences using the words they have written in the table.

- Check answers as a class. Learners then draw a picture to accompany their sentences.

> **Answers**
> Learners' own answers.

I can name things in a city.

Direct learners' attention to the self-evaluation question at the top of page 100. Ask them to think and answer. Emphasise the importance of giving an honest answer.

> **Answers**
> Learners' own answers.

> **Differentiated instruction**
>
> **Additional support and practice**
> - Ask learners to draw a map from their home to the school or another place in their city or town and then write sentences about it, using the language in the lesson to help them.
>
> **Extend and challenge**
> - Do **Photocopiable activity 17** with the learners as a class.

Lesson 2: Find out more

City living

Learner's Book pages: 124–125
Activity Book pages: 102–103

> **Lesson objectives**
>
> **Listening:** Listen to and understand key information. Listen to a conversation.
>
> **Speaking:** Practise topic vocabulary. Practise asking for and giving things.
>
> **Reading:** Read and understand factual information. Read a poem.
>
> **Writing:** Complete a dialogue.
>
> **Critical thinking:** Comparing size, comparing places.
>
> **Language focus:** Opposites, revision of present simple, revision of *there's*
>
> **Vocabulary:** *Live, buildings, great, ice cream seller, park, bakery, zoo, library, swimming pool, big, small, clean, dirty, litter, bin*

> **Materials:** Pictures to represent the vocabulary above; pencils and crayons, card, scissors, poster paper; boxes of different sizes; small toy cars and puppets.

Learner's Book

Warm up

- Ask learners: *What's the weather like today? Is it rainy or sunny?*

- Elicit answers from the class. Then they write in their weather journal and draw a picture.
- As a class, they recite the 'Days of the week' chant from **Lesson 1** of **Unit 8**.
- You could also ask the class to recite 'The Traffic Lights' poem from **Lesson 1** of this unit.

1 Before you read 84 [CD2 Track 31]

- Introduce the key vocabulary with the pictures. Say the words and ask learners to repeat.
- Ask learners to look at the photos, and listen to and read the texts.
- In pairs, learners discuss what things they can find in the places where they live.

> **Audioscript:** Track 84
> **Speaker:** *I like living in a city*
>
> I live in a city.
>
> It's a great place to live.
>
> There are tall buildings and short buildings.
>
> Some buildings have gardens on top!
>
> There's a park in my city.
>
> It's very pretty. It has flowers, a lake,
>
> and an ice cream seller!
>
> I like eating ice cream in the park.
>
> Sometimes parks and cities get dirty.
>
> We all need to keep our city clean.
>
> Don't forget to put your litter in a bin!

> **Suggested answers**
> Tall buildings and short buildings, a park with flowers and trees, a girl eating an ice cream and a rubbish bin.

2 Over to you

- Discuss the questions with learners. Focus on the pictures and introduce the vocabulary.
- Elicit as much vocabulary as possible from them and supply vocabulary as needed to do the task.
- **Critical thinking:** Ask learners to discuss in pairs what they like about living in their area. Is it similar to or different from a big city? Supply additional vocabulary as necessary.

> **Answers**
> Learners' own answers.

AB For further practice, see Activities 1, 2 and the **Challenge** in the Activity Book.

3 Let's buy an ice cream! 85 [CD2 Track 32]

- Explain the words *flavour* and *size*. Focus on the pictures. Ask learners to give more examples of things that are *big* and *small*, e.g. *an elephant, a frog.*
- Tell learners to listen to the dialogue. Play it a few times.
- Point out polite forms in the dialogue.

- In pairs, learners roleplay the dialogue, substituting the flavour and size of the ice creams.

> **Audioscript:** Track 85
>
> **Ice cream seller:** Hello! Would you like an ice cream?
>
> **Girl:** Yes, please! I'd like a banana ice cream.
>
> **Ice cream seller:** Big or small?
>
> **Girl:** Big, please.
>
> **Ice cream seller:** Here you are.
>
> **Girl:** Thank you!

 For further practice, see Activity 3 in the Activity Book.

4 Sing a city song 86 [CD2 Track 33]

- Tell learners that they are going to listen to a song about the city.
- Play the song a few times. Explain any vocabulary as necessary.
- Play the song again. Stop after each line for learners to repeat.
- Play the song again. Learners sing along.
- **Values:** The song is a good opportunity to discuss inclusion issues and equality. Is there ethnic variety in the area where learners live? How do they perceive people from other ethnic groups?

> **Audioscript:** Track 86
>
> ***I live in a city***
>
> I live in a city, yes I do,
>
> I live in a city, yes I do,
>
> I live in a city, yes I do,
>
> Made by human hands.
>
> Black hands, white hands, yellow and brown,
>
> All together built this town,
>
> Black hands, white hands, yellow and brown,
>
> All together makes the wheels go 'round.

👉 Wrap up

- Learners make a scale model of a city using boxes of different sizes. They can include small toy cars and puppets, and use an assortment of elements to make the trees, parks, etc.
- **Home–school link:** Learners ask their parents about the place where they lived when they were children. Was it a city or the countryside? What could they see, hear and do in that place? They can make notes and report back to the class. They can also teach the family the city song.

Activity Book

1 City places

- Focus on the pictures and elicit the words from the learners. They then write the words correctly in the Activity Book.

> **Answers**
> **1** park **2** road **3** zoo

2 Places near your home

- After learners have finished **Activity 1**, ask them to write which places are near their homes.
- Check answers as a class.

Challenge

- Ask learners to add two more places which are near their homes. Tell them to look at the **Picture dictionary** or the lesson for help if necessary.

> **Answers**
> Learners' own answers.

3 Let's buy an ice cream!

- Direct learners attention to the dialogue and the **Word box**. Using the pictures as help, learners choose words from the **Word box** to complete the dialogue.
- Ask pairs of learners to act out the dialogue in front of the class.

> **Answers**
> *like*
> *Yes*
> Learners' own answer
> *small*
> *please*
> *Thank you*

Challenge

- Read the clues aloud to the class. Refer learners to the Learner's Book where they will find the answers. Circulate to assist and check spelling.

> **Answers**
> *bin, lake, buildings*

I can name things in a city.

- Direct learners' attention to the self-evaluation question at the top of page 102. Ask them to think and answer. Emphasise the importance of giving an honest answer.

Differentiated instruction

Additional support and practice

- Ask learners to make word cards for key vocabulary. They choose two or three words and make illustrated word cards.

Extend and challenge

- Learners write more clues following the model of the mystery words in the Activity Book. They exchange the clues with other learners and solve the mystery words.

Lesson 3: Letters and sounds

-*y* endings

Learner's Book pages: 126–127
Activity Book pages: 104–105

Lesson objectives

Listening: Identify the sound of **-y** endings.

Speaking: Say a poem.

Reading: Recognise words with **-y** endings, read and follow instructions, read a story and answer questions about it.

Writing: Complete sentences, write rhyming words.

Critical thinking: Memorise and act out a poem, understand the concept of opposites.

Language focus: Identifying the sound of final **-y** ending words, identifying two-syllable words, opposite words

Vocabulary: *baby, cry, carry, fly, happy, sky, why*

Materials: Pictures or word cards to represent the vocabulary above.

Learner's Book

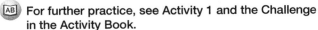 Warm up

- Ask learners: *What's the weather like today? Is it rainy or sunny?*
- Elicit answers from the class. Then they write in their weather journal and draw a picture.
- Write a few words with different sounds that the class has learned so far in the Learner's Book and ask learners to find words that rhyme.

1 Listen, say and clap 87 [CD2 Track 34]

- Focus on the two words: *my city.* Tell learners to clap the number of syllables in the two words.
- Play the first part of the audio while learners listen.
- Play the audio again. Learners clap as they listen.
- Discuss the number of syllables in each word in turn.

Audioscript: Track 87
Speaker: 1 my cit-y

Answers
My: one syllable.
City: two syllables.

2 Different sounds of -*y*

- Read the introductory sentence. Ask learners to repeat both words after you. Do they notice the difference? What are the sounds in each case?
- Focus on the one syllable words. Learners say each one, then proceed to the second set of words.

3 Which -*y* sound? 87 [CD2 Track 34]

- Tell learners you are going to listen to some more words. Play the second part of the audio once while learners listen.
- Play the audio again. This time learners count and clap the number of syllables in time with each word on the audio. They then decide which **-y** sound each word has.

Speaker: 3 baby
cry
carry
fly
happy
rainy
sky
why

Answers
Baby: two syllables [city]
Cry: one syllable [my]
Carry: two syllables [city]
Fly: one syllable [my]
Happy: two syllables [city]
Rainy: two syllables [city]
Sky: one syllable [my]
Why: one syllable [my]

[AB] **For further practice, see Activity 1 and the Challenge in the Activity Book.**

4 Which -*y* word?

- Direct learners' attention to the text and explain the activity.
- Learners work individually, completing the text with the missing words in their notebooks.

- When they have finished, they do peer correction with a partner, taking turns to read the sentences they have written.
- Check answers as a class by asking a few learners to come to the board and write their sentences.

> **Answers**
> 1 It's a **rainy** day. Don't forget your umbrella!
> 2 The **sky** is blue today.
> 3 **Why** are you sad?
> 4 I **cry** when I am sad.
> 5 I can **carry** all my teddies.
> 6 Look! I can **fly!**
> 7 I'm not sad. I'm **happy!**
> 8 A **baby** is very small.

5 Opposites

- **Critical thinking:** Ask learners about opposites in their own language, and explain that there are words with opposite meanings in English too.
- Focus on the words and the pictures. Read the words to the learners and ask them to repeat.
- Ask learners the question and elicit the answer. Do they know other opposites in English?

> **Answers**
> The opposite of big is **small**.

6 Opposites poem [CD2 Track 35]

- Tell learners that you are going to read a poem and they have to say the words that are missing. Tell them that each missing word rhymes with the last word of the previous line of the poem. Remind learners of rhyming words if necessary.
- Learners discuss the poem in pairs and use the pictures to help them complete the poem.
- Allow a few minutes for them to come up with the answers.
- Play the audio. Learners check if they were right.
- Then they match the verses with the correct pair of pictures.

> **Audioscript:** Track 88
> **Speaker:** *Opposites*
>
> The opposite of yes is no.
>
> The opposite of stop is go.
>
> The opposite of good is bad.
>
> The opposite of happy is sad.
>
> The opposite of hot is cold.
>
> The opposite of new is old.
>
> The opposite of wet is dry.
>
> The opposite of hello is goodbye.

> **Answers**
> The opposite of stop is go. (pictures c, d).
> The opposite of happy is sad. (pictures a, b)
> The opposite of new is old. (pictures g, h)
> The opposite of hello is goodbye. (pictures e, f)
>
> The words that rhyme are: *no/go, bad/sad, cold/old, dry/goodbye*

[AB] **For further practice, see Activity 2 in the Activity Book.**

7 Act it out 88 [CD2 Track 35]

- Play the 'Opposites' poem again. Ask learners to think of actions for the words in the poem.
- **Critical thinking:** Remind learners that they remember better if they make associations, e.g. associate the words with actions.
- Play the audio again. Learners act out the poem as they listen.

⤷ Wrap up

- Play an *Opposites* game with the words in the song. One learner says a word and the class has to provide the opposite.
- Pass out paper and pencils. Learners write their name at the top of the paper, then create a poem using words from this lesson. Collect, write the date on the back, and save in the learners' portfolios.
- **Home–school link:** Learners recite and teach the 'Opposites' poem to their family.

Activity Book

1 How many syllables?

- Remind learners of the rhyming words they studied at the beginning of the lesson.
- Focus on the pictures and the words, and say them together.
- Ask learners to classify the words. Check the answers as a class.

> **Answers**
> *baby:* two syllables
> *bakery:* three syllables
> *city:* two syllables
> *cry:* one syllable
> *fly:* one syllable

Challenge

- Direct learners to read the two lines from the city poem. Ask them to circle three words with the letter **y**. Then they write the three words and answer the question.

Answers			
1 city	**2** yes	**3** by	Different

2 Opposites crossword

- Explain the activity. Model one or two words with the class to make sure learners understand the mechanism of crossword solving.
- In pairs, learners work out the remaining words in the crossword. Check answers as a class.

Answers							
1 bad	**2** down	**3** new	**4** noisy	**5** big	**6** happy	**7** hot	**8** stop

I can read and write words that end in -*y*.
I can name opposites.

- Direct learners' attention to the self-evaluation questions at the top of page 104. Ask them to think and answer them. Emphasise the importance of giving an honest answer.

Answers
Learners' own answers.

Differentiated instruction
Additional support and practice

- Learners look for words they remember that end in -*y* from earlier in the Learner's Book. Encourage them to look at previous units. They choose a few and draw the pictures.

Extend and challenge

- 🗨 Ask learners to work in pairs and write a tongue twister using words from this lesson. Then they teach the tongue twister to the class.

Lesson 4: Use of English

This or *that*?

Learner's Book pages: 128–129
Activity Book pages: 106–107

Lesson objectives

Listening: Listen and understand, listen and check.

Speaking: Act out a conversation.

Reading: Read and complete sentences, read and answer questions.

Writing: Complete sentences, answer questions.

Language focus: Determiners *this/that*, pronouns *this/these*, questions: *What's this? What are these?*

Vocabulary: *round, clean, dirty, fix, mend*

Materials: Pictures or word cards to represent the vocabulary above.

Learner's Book

👉 Warm up

- Ask learners: *What's the weather like today? Is it rainy or sunny?*
- Elicit answers from the class. Then they write in their weather journal and draw a picture.
- In groups, learners act out the poem in **Lesson 3**.

1 The Fix-it kids 89 [CD2 Track 36]

- Look at the picture. Remind learners of the words *fix* and *mend,* and their meanings.
- Tell learners you are going to listen to two children who are mending things.
- Ask learners to listen and point to the things the children say.
- Play the audio a few times for learners to understand, then ask them to fill in the missing words in the conversations. They write them in their notebooks.

Audioscript: Track 89

Child A: My friend and I like fixing things.

Child B: We are the Fix-it kids!

Child A: This ball is round.

Child B: That ball is flat.

Child A: This bucket is clean.

Child B: That bucket is dirty.

Child A: This chair has four legs.

Child B: That chair has three legs.

Child A: This frog is green.

Child B: That frog is grey.

Child A: This teddy bear has eyes.

Child B: That teddy bear doesn't have eyes.

Answers	
My friend and I like fixing things.	We are the Fix-it kids!
This ball is round.	That ball is **flat**.
This bucket is clean.	That bucket is **dirty**.
This chair has **four** legs.	**That** chair has three legs.
This frog is **green**.	That frog is **grey**.
This teddy bear has eyes.	**That** teddy bear doesn't have eyes.

2 🗨 Act it out

- In pairs, learners re-read the conversations and act them out.
- Ask more confident learners to act out their conversations for the class.

AB For further practice, see Activities 1 and 2 in the Activity Book.

3 Play a game: What's this? What are these?

- Focus on the picture and explain the game. Read through the instructions and model first to make the rules of the game clear.
- Tell learners to play in pairs and to look at the pictures in the **Picture dictionary** if they need help for answers.

4 Words I know

- Read the questions with the class. Ask learners to reflect on them.
- You may wish to ask learners to write in their notebooks the words they have most difficulty with.
- Emphasise the importance of giving an honest answer in this task.

> **Answers**
> Learners' own answers.

Wrap up

- Ask learners to take turns asking the class questions about classroom objects, e.g. *What are these?* The class answers, e.g. *They're chairs.*
- **Home–school link:** Learners teach the game to their family and play at home.

Activity Book

1 *This* or *that*?

- Explain the use of *this* and *that.* Focus on the **Language tip box** and read the examples with the class.
- Give more examples using objects around the class. Invite more confident learners to give examples too.
- Explain the activity. Model the first sentence and ask learners to proceed independently.
- Circulate helping as necessary. Check as a class.

> **Answers**
> Learners' own answers.

2 Let's go to the zoo!

- Ask learners what animals they can see in the zoo. Elicit a few examples.
- Focus on the **Language tip box** and explain the use of *this* and *these.*
- Give more examples using objects around the class. Invite learners to give examples.
- Point to the questions and ask the class. Elicit answers from learners.
- Ask learners to write the answers in their Activity Book. Check answers as a class.

> **Answers**
> 1 This is a *deer.*
>
> 2 What is *this?*
>   *This is a turtle.*
>
> 3 *These* are *pandas.*
>
> 4 *What are these?*
>   *These are elephants.*

I can talk about things using *this* and *that*.

- Direct learners' attention to the self-evaluation question at the top of page 106. Ask them to think and answer. Emphasise the importance of giving an honest answer.

> **Answers**
> Learners' own answers.

Differentiated instruction

Additional support and practice

- Learners make sentence cards using those words they had more difficulty remembering. They display their cards and read the sentences to the class.

Extend and challenge

- In pairs, ask learners to write conversations following the model of **Activity 1** in the Learner's Book using vocabulary from the **Picture dictionary**.

Lesson 5: Read and respond

Learner's Book pages: 130–133
Activity Book pages: 108–109

Lesson objectives

Listening: Listen to a poem.

Speaking: Discuss a poem, act out the poem, describe locations.

Reading: Read a poem, do a reading comprehension exercise.

Writing: Choose words to complete sentences.

Critical thinking: Understand the difference between British and American English, observe details and discuss them.

Language focus: Revision of present simple and continuous, revision of *can*

Vocabulary: *people, sidewalk, subway, underneath, store, elevator, grumpy, smile, laugh, crowd*

Sight words: *people, with, on* and *in*

Materials: Pictures or word cards to represent the vocabulary above; a map of the world or globe; glue, scissors, pencils and crayons, A3 sheets of paper, old magazines.

Learner's Book

☞ Warm up

- Ask learners: *What's the weather like today? Is it rainy or sunny?*
- Elicit answers from the class. Then they write in their weather journal and draw a picture.
- Ask learners to remind you what they can see, hear and smell in the city. Elicit examples from them for each sense.

☞ Word game

- Play a few rounds of *Simon says* to introduce the following vocabulary:
  Walk fast, walk slow.
  Walk up and down the room.
  Let's hurry!
  Walk singly (one by one)
  Walk in a crowd
  Walk in front of me, in back of me
  Smile, laugh, be grumpy (frown and make a 'go away' gesture)

1 Before you read 90 [CD2 Track 37]

- Open books at page 130. Focus on the introductory sentences. On the map or globe, ask learners to show you where the United States of America and Britain are.
- **Critical thinking:** Explain that people in Britain and the USA both speak English but there are differences in the way they speak. Give other examples of similar countries; for example, in Spain and in Latin American countries (except for Brazil) people speak Spanish, but there are differences in the way they speak. The same happens with Portugal and Brazil.
- Focus on the words in the lists and read them with the class. Explain meanings as necessary or show pictures.
- Tell learners that they are going to read a poem. Focus on the **About the author** box. Do they know the name of any other poets?
- Read the title. Tell learners look at the pictures to predict what the poem will be about.
- Play the recording once. Learners listen and follow in their books to check if they were right.
- Play the recording a few more times. Pause after each verse for learners to repeat. Check for correct pronunciation.

Audioscript: Track 90
See Learner's Book pages 130–132.

2 💬 Picture search

- Focus on the questions. Read and model the first example for learners. They look at the pictures, discuss their answers in pairs and point at the people in the picture.
- They then proceed to complete the task with their partner.
- **Critical thinking:** In this activity, learners not only develop their observation skills, they also show understanding of the vocabulary they have learned and make mental associations, equating image with meaning.

> **Answers**
> All the images mentioned in the exercise are in each picture.

3 Where is the goose?

- Now tell learners to find the goose in every picture in the poem. Pretend to be the goose and ask: *Where am I? Am I on the bus?* Learners answer.

> **Answers**
> In the first picture the goose is on the bus.
> In the second picture the goose is on a train.
> In the third picture the goose is waiting next to the traffic lights.
> In the fourth picture the goose is sitting at a table under an umbrella.

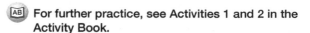 For further practice, see Activities 1 and 2 in the Activity Book.

4 💬 Perform the poem

- Read the instructions with the learners. Divide the class into groups and assign a verse to each.
- They practise their lines and draw a picture, then perform the whole poem as a class, miming as necessary.

AB For further practice, see Activities 3 and 4 in the Activity Book.

Words to remember

- Write the words *people, with, on* and *in* on the board.
- Learners look for the sight words in the text. How many times do they see the word? Tell them to count on their fingers. Ask them to read the sentences where the words appear with a partner.

> **Answers**
> - *people* appears 19 times
> - *with* appears twice
> - *on* appears 4 times
> - *in* appears 6 times

Wrap up

- In small groups, learners make a city collage with pictures from old magazines. Then they write a short poem about their city following the model in the lesson.
- **Home–school link:** Learners teach the poem to their family.

Activity Book

1 Sing a song of people

- Tell learners to read the poem and write the missing word at the end of each verse.
- When they have finished, they take turns to read the completed verses to the class.

> **Answers**
> *us, round, go, you*

2 Match the pictures

- Focus on the pictures. Ask learners to match them to the correct verse of the poem. Check answers as a class.

> **Answers**
> d   c   a   b

3 Vehicles in the city

- Focus on the pictures of the city in the Learner's Book, page 122. Ask: *What vehicles can you see?* Elicit answers from the class.
- Learners then write the words on the lines in the Activity Book.

> **Answers**
> Learners' own answers.

4 Where is the goose?

- Revise prepositions by putting objects in different places around the room. Ask: *Where's the…? / Where are the…?* Learners answer.
- Focus on each picture in the activity. Ask: *Where's the goose?* Tell learners to answer using words from the word box. Elicit answers.
- Tell learners to write a sentence to say where the goose is. Check answers as a class.

> **Answers**
> Learners' own answers.

I can name things in a city.

- Focus on the self-evaluation question at the top of page 108. Ask learners to think and answer. Emphasise the importance of giving an honest answer.

> **Answers**
> Learners' own answers.

Differentiated instruction

Additional support and practice

- Ask learners to write a new verse for 'Sing a song of people'. They draw a picture to illustrate their verse.

Extend and challenge

- Ask learners to look for information about the United States of America, e.g. the capital, animals and plants, interesting places. They can cut out pictures or print images from websites to do this. They then make illustrated word cards and place them on the map.

Lesson 6: Choose a project

What can you see, hear and do in a city?

Learner's Book pages: 134–135
Activity Book pages: 110–111

Lesson objectives

Listening: Listen to comprehension items in the Activity Book quiz.

Speaking: Present your project to the class.

Reading: Read instructions, read sentences to do a matching exercise in the Activity Book quiz.

Writing: Write a poem, draw and label a city map, write in an opposites book, write words in the Activity Book quiz.

Language focus: Unit 9 Review

Materials:

A Write a poem: Sheets of paper, pencils and crayons.

B Draw a city map: Pencils and crayons, sheets of A3 paper.

C Make an opposites book: Sheets of paper, pencils and crayons, old magazines, glue, scissors, stapler.

A copy of **Photocopiable activity 18** for each learner.

Learner's Book

Warm up

- Ask learners: *What's the weather like today? Is it rainy or sunny?*
- Elicit answers from the class. Then they write in their weather journal and draw a picture.

Choose a project

- Learners choose an end-of-unit project to work on. Look at the learner-made samples and help them choose. Move the children into groups depending on their choices. Provide materials.

A Write a poem
- Read the instructions in the Learner's Book. Explain any vocabulary as necessary to learners.
- Learners write their poem, copy it on a sheet of paper and draw a picture to illustrate it.

B Draw a city map
- Give learners sheets of A3 paper, and pencils and crayons. Tell them they can also use pictures cut out from magazines on their map.
- They draw their map including the items indicated in the book.
- Learners label their map and show it to the class.

C Make an opposites book
- Guide learners through the instructions in the Learner's Book and give them a set of materials to make the book.
- They make their lists of opposites and draw the pictures, or use pictures cut out from magazines, to illustrate the book.
- They make the covers and staple the sheets together.
- **Informal assessment opportunity:** Circulate as learners work. Informally assess their receptive and productive language skills. Check for correct pronunciation and spelling of new vocabulary. Ask questions. You may want to take notes on their responses.
- If possible, leave the learner projects on display for a short while, then consider filing the projects, photos or scans of the work, in learners' portfolios. Write the date on the work.

Look what I can do!
- Review the *I can …* statements. Learners demonstrate what they can do.

AB For further practice, see the quiz in the Activity Book.

Activity Book

Unit 9 Quiz: Look what I can do!

Listen 99 [CD2 Track 46]
- For items 1–5, learners listen to the audio and tick the correct picture. Do the first item as a class. Play the audio several times.

Audioscript: Track 99

Narrator: 1

Speaker 1: This is a busy road. There's a lot of traffic today!

Speaker 2: Yes, look at all the cars and buses.

Narrator: 2

Speaker 1: I'd like an ice cream, please.

Speaker 2: What flavour?

Speaker 1: Banana.

Speaker 2: Here you are!

Speaker 1: Thank you.

Narrator: 3

Speaker 1: I'd like to buy some bread.

Speaker 2: OK. Here's a bakery. Let's go in.

Narrator: 4

Speaker: There's a park in my city. It has a lake and flowers.

Narrator: 5

Speaker: That teddy bear is big.

Answers
1 b   2 a   3 c   4 b   5 b

Read and write
- For items 6 and 7, learners read the sentence and tick the correct pictures. For items 8 and 9, learners write the words to go with the pictures.

Answers
6 a
7 b
8 *sky*
9 *city*

- Make up a certificate for each learner using **Photocopiable activity 18**.
Don't forget to celebrate their achievements!

Unit 6

Photocopiable activity 12: Project A – Do a class survey

Do you like this _____?		_____	_____	_____	_____
Draw and write	Yes, I do.				
	No, I don't.				
Draw and write	Yes, I do.				
	No, I don't.				

Photocopiable activity 13: Make a helicopter

1 Cut out the paper helicopter shape.

2 Cut on the solid lines. Fold on the broken lines.

3 Attach the paper clip.

4 Fly your helicopter.

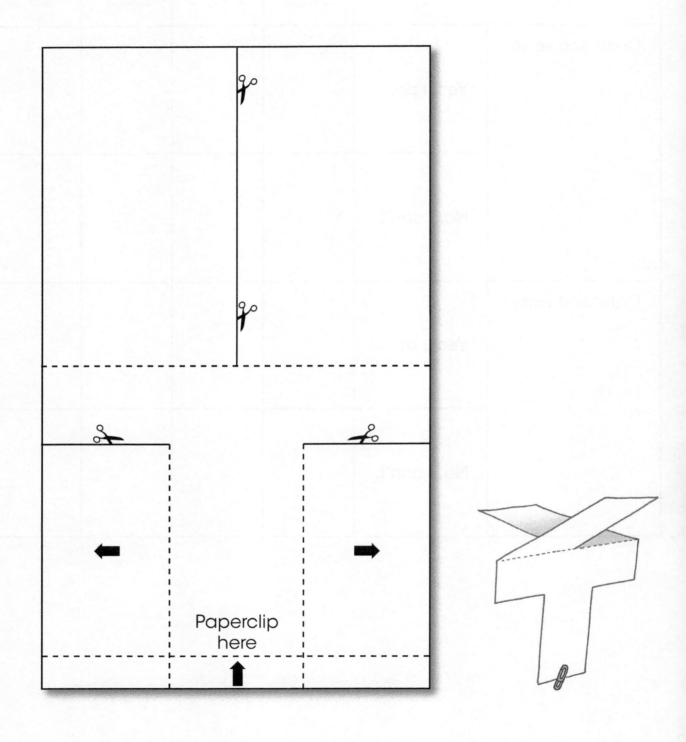

Paperclip here

Photocopiable activity 14: Numbers extension 20–30

Colour and count.

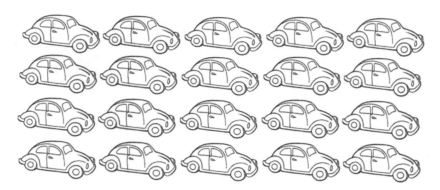

Colour 5 cars blue.

Colour 5 cars green.

Colour 5 cars red.

Colour 5 cars orange.

Count the cars.

How many cars? _____

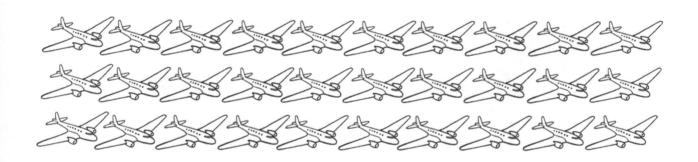

Colour 10 planes yellow.

Colour 10 planes black.

Colour 10 planes purple.

Count the planes.

How many planes? _____

Photocopiable activity 15: Puppets for *The song of the toad* story

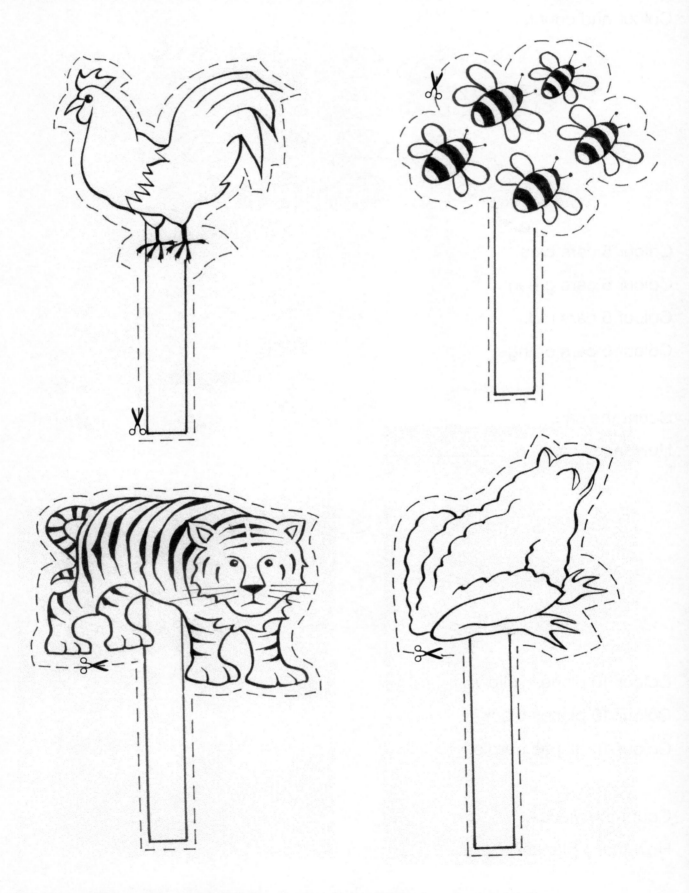

**Photocopiable activity 16: Project C – Do an experiment:
Does your boat float?**

Does Boat A float?		
	Yes, it does.	**No, it doesn't.**
with 0 coins?		
with 2 coins?		
with 5 coins?		
with 10 coins?		

Does Boat B float?		
	Yes, it does.	**No, it doesn't.**
with 0 coins?		
with 2 coins?		
with 5 coins?		
with 10 coins?		

Photocopiable activity 17: Numbers extension 30–100

Write the missing numbers.

30	31	___	33	34	35	36	37	___	39
40	___	42	___	44	___	46	47	48	49
50	51	52	53	___	55	___	57	___	59
60	61	___	___	64	65	___	67	68	___
___	71	___	73	74	___	76	___	78	79
80	___	___	83	___	85	___	87	88	___
90	91	___	___	94	95	96	97	___	___
100									

What is your favourite number between 30 and 100? Write it here: _____ .

End of book

Photocopiable activity 18: Congratulations certificate for completing Stage 1 of *Cambridge Global English*

Congratulations!

You have completed Stage 1 of *Cambridge Global English*.

Name: _____

Class: _____

Teacher: _____

Cambridge Global English Stage 1 Teacher's Resource © Cambridge University Press 2016   **149**

Photocopiable word lists

Unit 1

chair	clock	computer
crayon	duck	lunchbox
rabbit	school	squirrel
swim	whiteboard	

Unit 2

bread	brother	father
mother	noodles	pineapple
sister	soup	strawberry
yogurt		

Unit 3

bird	bounce	catch
ear	kick	knee
nose	shoulders	throw
water		

Unit 4

circle	clown	jacket
quilt	shirt	shoemaker
shoes	skirt	square
triangle		

Unit 5

carrot	chick	farmer
ground	lettuce	onions
peppers	seed	tractor
vegetable		

Unit 6

elephant	eyes	hard
ice cream	juicy	mouth
saxophone	touch	wiggly
worm		

Cambridge Global English Stage 1 Teacher's Resource © Cambridge University Press 2016

Unit 7

bicycle	buckle up	bumpy
drive	hydrofoil	shape
skateboard	town	tricycle
wheelchair		

Unit 8

crocodile	flowers	puddle
rainy	scream	snow
sunny	Thursday	umbrella
Wednesday	whale	

bakery	buildings	crowd
grumpy	laugh	litter
park	sidewalk	subway
traffic		